University of Cambridge Department of Applied Economics
OCCASIONAL PAPER 43

THE STRUCTURE OF INDUSTRY IN THE EEC:
AN INTERNATIONAL COMPARISON

The Structure of Industry in the EEC

KENNETH D. GEORGE and T.S. WARD

CAMBRIDGE UNIVERSITY PRESS
Cambridge
London : New York : Melbourne

Published by the Syndics of the Cambridge University Press
The Pitt Building, Trumpington Street, Cambridge CB2 1RP
Bentley House, 200 Euston Road, London NW1 2DB
32 East 57th Street, New York, NY 10022, USA
296 Beaconsfield Parade, Middle Park, Melbourne 3206, Australia

© Department of Applied Economics 1975

hard covers ISBN 0 521 20867 X
paperback ISBN 0 521 09978 1

First published 1975

Set by E.W.C. Wilkins Ltd., London and Northampton,
and printed in Great Britain at the University Printing House,
Cambridge (Euan Phillips, University Printer).

Contents

		Page	
	Preface		vii
1	**Introduction**		1
2	**International comparisons of industrial structure**		5
	1. Previous studies		5
	2. The data		10
	(a) 1963 Census of Production comparisons		10
	(b) Method of estimating concentration ratios and average sizes of firm and plant from size distributions		13
3	**Concentration and the size of enterprises**		15
	1. Concentration ratios		15
	2. Concentration and industry size		22
	3. The average size of the largest enterprises		23
	4. The size of firms and industries		23
	5. Concentration, firm size and industry size		24
	6. Summary and interpretation of main conclusions		25
	Appendix 3.1. Ratios of industry size and of the average size of the 4 largest firms, UK, Germany and France		27
	Appendix 3.2. UK–West German industry comparisons		28
4	**Comparisons of plant size**		29
	1. Average plant size		29
	2. Plant concentration ratios		31
	3. Plant size and industry size		36
	4. Plant concentration ratios and industry size		37
	5. Further analysis of plant size – the UK and West Germany 1958 to 1968		37
	6. Size of plant and output per head		43
	7. Summary of main conclusions		44
	Appendix 4.1. Average size of the 20 largest plants by industry, UK, Germany, France and Italy, 1963		45
	Appendix 4.2. 4-firm and 4-plant concentration ratios, UK, Germany and France, 1963		46
	Appendix 4.3. The 1958, 1963 and 1968 comparisons of plant size by industry order, UK and West Germany		47
	Appendix 4.4. Plants employing 1000 or more, UK and West Germany, 1958, 1963 and 1968		48

		Page	
5	**The largest industrial corporations**		49
	1. Aggregate concentration in the industrial sector		49
	2. Concentration amongst the top 100 EEC companies		51
	(a) Introduction		51
	(b) Changes in concentration 1962 to 1972		53
	3. Composition of the largest companies by country and industry		54
	(a) Composition by country		54
	(b) Composition by industry		55
6	**Changes in output, employment and labour productivity in manufacturing, UK and West Germany**		60
	1. Introduction		60
	2. Previous studies		60
	3. The UK performance		65
	4. The UK–West Germany comparison		66
	Appendix 6.1. List of industries in regression analysis		73
	List of works cited		74

Preface

This Paper is the first stage of a Social Science Research Council financed project on 'Anti-trust and Industrial Policy : UK and EEC'. The research was undertaken largely during the first half of 1973 when both authors were still in Cambridge.

Mr. Roger Tarling and Mr. Alan Hughes read an earlier draft of the Paper, and we are most grateful to them for their constructive criticisms.

The many computations were carried out by Mrs. Marion Hughes, Miss Diana Day and Mrs. Mavis Barnett with their usual skill and accuracy; thanks are due to all three and to Mrs. Patricia Buckingham who typed the Paper through its various stages with great patience and efficiency.

Cardiff	KDG
Cambridge	TSW |//

December, 1974.

1
Introduction

The basic object of this paper is to compare certain important aspects of the structure of industry in the UK with that prevailing in the largest three other member-countries of the European Economic Community. Of the latter, principal attention is focused upon West Germany, which is after all the UK's main competitor for a great many manufactured goods and the industrial structure of which provides perhaps the most suitable yardstick for judging that of the UK.

Comparative studies of this nature are of very recent origin and although there has been some upsurge in the amount of work done in the past few years, it nevertheless remains true that the information available at the present time is of a rather piece-meal and limited character. Yet research into this area represents an essential preliminary step to assessing the influence of industrial structure on economic performance, a factor which has received scant attention in comparative international studies of growth and productivity. Such research would hopefully provide a more satisfactory guide to the policy-maker, concerned with maintaining and manipulating structural developments, than has existed in the past.

In the UK in particular, the last ten years has seen much more active and wide-ranging attempts by government to exercise some control over the size of firms and the degree of industrial concentration than ever before. However the action taken, whether in the form of promoting mergers and larger enterprises *via* the Industrial Reorganisation Corporation or of deciding the desirability of proposed amalgamations *via* the machinery established by the 1965 Monopolies and Mergers Act, has often rested on rather shaky premises to say the least. References have all too frequently been made, for instance, to British organisations being too small to be able to compete satisfactorily with their foreign counterparts without there being any systematic or rigorous attempt to justify such an assertion. Indeed policy has been implemented on the basis of this type of supposition as if it were a self-evident fact. Most notably the IRC was established precisely because it was considered that 'there was a need for more concentration and rationalisation to promote the greater efficiency and international competitiveness of British industry.'[1] This statement was made in the context of expanding trade with Western Europe and potential British entry into the EEC, yet it was made at a time when almost nothing was known about how British firms and plants generally compared in size with their competitors on the continent, let alone about how size and efficiency were related.

While knowledge has expanded since, it still lags far behind what is necessary to

---

1   Industrial Reorganisation Corporation, *First Report and Accounts*, HMSO., May 1968, p. 5.

implement policy with any degree of confidence, even though the IRC is no longer in existence. Moreover most research effort in this country has been devoted to unravelling structural developments and to giving a more complete picture of the prevailing features of manufacturing industry in the UK. The primary aim of this paper is simply to set this picture in an international context, rather than to pursue at all fully the association between structural characteristics and economic performance.

However some consideration is given to the experience of UK industries in terms of labour productivity movements and output growth over the post-war period, and this is related to the record of the equivalent industries in West Germany. This is intended mainly as background information and no attempt is made at a systematic evaluation of the effect of differing degrees of concentration or plant size, for instance, on productivity change. Indeed it is not immediately apparent what one would expect to observe in this regard, if only because by and large the comparative statistics available on industry structure in the two countries relate to one particular year and, except for plant size, it is not possible as yet to get an indication of changes through time, which are likely to be of considerable importance. Moreover movements in labour productivity are only one possible measure of relative performance and, in this context, not necessarily the most appropriate. It is largely left open to the reader to form his own judgement on these matters if he has a mind to, and it is hoped to explore this area more fully in future research, in which it is intended to select a limited number of trades for detailed examination.

Outline of analysis

The study concentrates on analysing what can be gleaned from published statistics, principally those collected in the periodic Censuses of Production as regards the UK and those compiled in the 1963 industrial enquiry with respect to the EEC countries.

The central part of the study – chapters 2 to 4 – consists of an examination of certain aspects of industrial structure in the UK and in West Germany, France and Italy, which can be derived from the official sources noted above. The biggest problem here is to reconcile differences in classification between the UK Census data on the one hand and the EEC data on the other. While this was found to be impossible for all industry categories, nevertheless a fairly satisfactory degree of comparability can be achieved for over 40 trades, which cover about half of all manufacturing activities. Inter-country comparisons are made of the average size and relative importance of the largest four enterprises and the largest 20 plants, as calculated from the published frequency distributions. This exercise is performed, unavoidably, in terms of employment, this being the only variable on which the necessary details were collected by the EEC enquiry. Fortunately other studies have generally come to the conclusion that the results are not greatly affected by the measure chosen for comparison, though admittedly such studies have mostly been concerned with the relative concentration of industries within a single country. Whether the same is true if the comparison is extended to more than one country has to remain an open question.

While the main object of this section is simply to compare concentration ratios and the size of firms and plants in UK industries as opposed to those in Germany, France and Italy, a related aim is to reassess the findings of the very few previous studies of comparative structure. The most notable features to emerge from these are, first, that concentration ratios tend to vary inversely with the size of market and, secondly, that the size of plant and enterprise tends to be directly related to market size.

The above analysis, as we have mentioned, is restricted in the main to the situation as it was in 1963, and no information is as yet available which enables us to compare changes in concentration or plant size over time for these four countries and at this level of disaggregation. This is clearly unfortunate as such changes might well modify any conclusions – as to the relative degree of competition in the four countries for example – which appear to be implied by the picture at one point in time. In other words, the dynamic factors at work are as much, if not more, worthy of consideration as the static situation in a given year. For instance there is no doubt that the period since 1963 has been one in which major changes have occurred in the degree of concentration in British industry as is reflected in the big increase in merger activity among large manufacturing companies. At the same time, there is evidence that the UK has not been alone in experiencing such a merger boom and that in particular West Germany also experienced a high level of expenditure on acquisitions in the late 1960's. However, we are able to do something in this direction at a more aggregative level for the UK and West Germany as far as industrial plants are concerned. Statistics published in the periodic UK Censuses of Production and in the annual German *Statistisches Jahrbuch* enable at least an examination to be made of the size of plant by industry order in each of the three years 1958, 1963 and 1968 and give an indication therefore of changes over this period in the two countries. In addition, by using the information contained in the 1967 German Census of Production and the 1968 UK Census, we are able to compare net output per head for plants of different size in the countries in question. This gives some indication of the comparative importance of increasing returns, as well as of the disparity in the pattern of labour productivity between the UK and Germany at the industry order level.

In chapter 5 a further glimpse of changes which have taken place in industrial structure is obtained. Although the necessary Census data are not available, we can nevertheless get some, albeit limited, insight into changes in aggregate concentration across EEC member countries from the details published in the Fortune directory of the 200 (now 300) largest companies outside the US. This gives the rank order of enterprises in terms of their dollar-equivalent sales and allows us to compile a list of the largest 100 European industrial companies, on this basis, for each of the years 1962 to 1972. An analysis is then made of changes in each country's representation in the top 100, in the industrial composition of this group and in the degree of concentration within it. Even though the data used are far from ideal, and dollar sales may not be the most appropriate measure of firm size, especially as very diverse activities are involved, the exercise provides tentative answers to such questions as whether the major British companies tend to be smaller than their European counterparts, whether they are competing in the same trades, and whether the very largest concerns show a tendency to increase in relative importance.

Finally, chapter 6 examines the performance of UK manufacturing industries in relation to that of a number of other countries, though most attention is focused upon a comparison with West Germany. This makes use of the data contained in the

United Nations, *Growth of World Industry*, which relate broadly to two-digit industries or what in the UK would be industry orders. An attempt is also made to check the findings which emerge against the experience of more narrowly defined trade groups, as derived from the statistics compiled by domestic sources. The main focal point of this part of the study is the relationship between changes in output and output per man, which has generally been found to be a pronounced feature of inter-industry studies and indeed is evident in comparisons made of different countries. The results obtained show a number of interesting differences between the UK and West Germany and open up avenues which are clearly worth exploring in future research.

It should be emphasised again that the main objective of this Paper is descriptive rather than analytical. Many of the findings which are presented clearly point to the need for more detailed investigation before any serious attempt at analysis can be made.

2
International comparisons of industrial structure

In this and the following two chapters we are concerned with a comparative analysis of industrial structure. Before turning to the results of our own research, however, we first summarise briefly the main findings of previous work in this field, and secondly, examine the data problems involved in our study.

1. Previous studies

There is no doubt that the publication in 1969 of the 1963 industrial enquiry in the EEC countries has been the significant factor underlying the greatly increased number of recent studies into comparative industrial structure. Up to that year, almost no work at all had been done on comparing concentration or size of plant as between countries, or indeed was possible to perform. There are a number of exceptions, notably the pioneering effort of Bain (1966) in the mid-1960's to undertake an international comparison of these items, although his work as much highlights the practical difficulty of making such a study as anything else.[1] In addition, a few attempts had been made to compare manufacturing structure in the UK and the US, particularly in terms of concentration. These include those by P. Sargant Florence (1953) for 1935, and P. Pashigian (1968) for 1951. More recently Sawyer (1971) and Shepherd (1972) have examined the same theme from 1963 data. The general findings of these studies are that concentration tends to be higher in the UK than the US and that the concentration ranking of industries tends to be similar in both countries. The former finding has been explained in terms of differences in market size (by Pashigian in particular) although Shepherd has argued that if 'regional' industries (those where the market of particular firms is largely confined to a certain region in which they enjoy monopoly powers) are excluded and if differences in the importance of imports are explicitly taken into account, the picture is reversed, the US emerging with higher concentration than the UK.[2]

Few studies have attempted to compare the UK with other Western European countries, though in view of the expanding trade with this area and, more especially, the entry of the UK into the EEC, such a comparison seems more relevant than one vis à vis the US. An exception was an attempt by Ray (1966) to compare the sizes

---

[1] The countries included in Bain's study were US, UK, Canada, France, Sweden, Italy, India and Japan.

[2] In addition to Shepherd (1972) see the interchange between him and Sawyer in *Oxford Economics Papers*, Nov. 1972.

of the largest UK plants with those in German industries. This was based on Census of Production data for 1958 and details published annually in the German statistical yearbook (*Statistisches Jahrbuch für die Bundesrepublik Deutschland*) on the size distribution of plants. From these sources it is possible to compare plant sizes approximately by industry order, but owing to the lack of a breakdown for Germany at the very top end of the scale, the largest published size class consists of plants employing a thousand or more. Ray's point of comparison centred upon the average employment size of plants with a thousand or more persons engaged in the two countries in 1958, and he concluded that these large plants were bigger on average in Germany than in Britain, and moreover that this applied *a fortiori* to those industries which exported a relatively large proportion of their output (vehicles, chemicals and metals in particular). However, this method of analysis is clearly liable to be misleading. Specifically, it takes no account of the potential differences in the number of plants which are defined as large as between the two countries, and it is interesting to note that Britain possessed a greater proportion of these than Germany in the year in question. An alternative analysis of this data is contained in the present study, an attempt being made to compare the average sizes of a common number of plants in each country. This rests on the convenient finding that conclusions as to relative size drawn from a comparison of n plants or firms are not greatly altered if k units are taken instead. (For example, Phlips's results show hardly any reversal of relative size as between France and Italy if the largest 8, 20 or 50 plants or enterprises are adopted as a basis of comparison instead of the largest 4.[1] This finding is supported by other studies, and by our results for the UK and Germany.) Furthermore, the publication of details of the size distribution of plants in the UK in 1963 and 1968 enables us to examine relative changes in plant size over the period 1958 to 1968.

In addition to comparing size, Ray also briefly examined differences in net output per head in the two countries as between plants of different size in 1954, and found a much greater tendency for this to increase with size – especially at the very top end of the scale – in Germany than in Britain. This finding has been re-examined using 1967 Census information for Germany and 1968 Census details for the UK.

Other recent studies have, however, included the UK in analyses of concentration and plant size over a number of countries, without focusing explicit attention upon comparing the British pattern with that shown by other countries. In addition to the Bain study noted above, these include the work done by Pryor (1972*a* and 1972*b*) and Scherer (1973). Pryor has conducted international comparisons of both concentration ratios and plant size. The former study is based on data for 12 countries, including the UK, Germany and France, for a period in the mid-1960's. For Britain, however, the Evely and Little calculations for 1951 are used and this is clearly likely to represent an important, if unacknowledged, qualification to the comparative results obtained for this country. The four-firm concentration ratios for a varying number of four-digit industries for each country are compared with the US ratios and a weighted average ratio derived with the US equal to 100. From this it emerges that concentration ratios are similar as between the large industrial

---

1 See L. Phlips (1971).

countries and lower than for smaller countries.[1] In addition, Pryor found not only the rank-order of industries to be similar in terms of concentration as between countries, but also that most countries had concentration ratios which were roughly the same with respect to particular industries, although interestingly the UK was something of an exception to this finding.

The second Pryor study compares establishment size in manufacturing across 23 countries using census data. The main findings to emerge are: first, that the relative size-ranking of average establishment size across industries (measured in three ways: the arithmetic mean, the Niehans index, and the percentage of the labour force engaged in establishments employing a thousand or more) are similar as between countries, which suggests the importance of technological considerations; secondly, that there is a positive relationship between establishment size and the size of the domestic market. The latter is rationalised in terms of three main factors. First, establishment size is limited by the costs incurred in overcoming environmental factors such as transport costs and barriers to foreign trade. The smaller the domestic market and the greater the barriers to trade the smaller will establishment size tend to be. Secondly, there are considerations of enterprise administration costs. Because of lower unit costs of co-ordination, etc., establishments in multi-establishment enterprises are larger than single-establishment enterprises, and the larger the enterprise the larger tend to be the different establishments composing it. The degree of multi-establishment enterprise is in turn related to the size of the domestic market, so that a positive association between the size of establishment and size of domestic market can be expected. Thirdly, import substitution policies are alleged to have led to the inefficient production of many goods, though this view, unsubstantiated as it is, is open to some debate. Pryor's argument is that such policies tend to be more important in smaller countries more dependent on foreign trade, so that establishment size may be linked with the size of the economy through governmental balance of payments policies.

Interestingly the UK is shown to have larger plants in manufacturing, on average, in 1958 than Germany in 1962 by all three measures used.[2] In addition, the size of French manufacturing establishments is reported as being lower than that of either the UK and Germany on the basis of two of the three measures, and the size of Italian plants as being below that of the French.[3]

The third study referred to above is that by Scherer, which attempts to explain industrial plant sizes for 12 selected, rather narrowly defined, industries across six countries, including the UK, France and Germany. The average plant size of those plants accounting for the top 50 per cent of output, or employment where an output

1   Britain is reported as being more concentrated than Germany or France, which have very similar values. This finding becomes even more noteworthy if account is taken of the widespread increase in concentration which occurred between 1951 and 1963.

2   Incidentally, Pryor's figure for the percentage of the total labour force engaged in establishments employing a thousand or more in Germany is something of a mystery and seems much too low according to our calculations, which yield 36.7 per cent instead of 27.7 per cent.

3   The Niehans index, however, produces some strange results, indicating French plants as being largest of all of the countries studied, including the US, and Belgian plants as being third largest overall behind these two countries. If correctly calculated, these figures must cast considerable doubt on the usefulness of this index.

measure is not available, in each of the industries in 1967, as derived from national census data (1963 for the UK, 1966 for France), are compared and related to estimates of minimal optimal production scale (which were found to be fairly uniform as between countries in 1965), as suggested by interviews with manufacturers in the various countries. In terms of employment, Scherer found that the US, UK, and Germany possessed similar plant sizes on average, on his definition, while French plants were slightly smaller. The ratio of the average size of the top 50 per cent of plants, in terms of estimated output, to the minimal optimal scale, is related to relative market size, unit transport costs, concentration, annual production growth, the excess of costs at one third minimal optimal scale over those at minimal optimal scale, and population density. A strong positive association emerged between the dependent variable and both market size and concentration, the former relationship supporting Pryor's findings and the latter being especially marked for Europe.

There are, however, a number of questions which might be raised with respect to Scherer's analysis. In particular, he has covered only a small proportion of manufacturing; secondly, the concept of minimal optimal scale and its actual estimation is open to criticism. One might ask, in fact, why the concept has been incorporated in the analysis at all, in view of the assumption that it does not vary between countries. As it stands, the measure does not have any obvious advantages over a direct comparison of actual size of plant.[1]

Finally, two recent studies have focused attention on comparative industrial structure within the countries of the original EEC, deriving data from the 1963 EEC industrial enquiry. The first of these, undertaken by Horowitz (1970) is an entropy approach to the analysis of concentration in 26, 2-digit industries in each of the six EEC member countries. The conclusions to emerge are that there are strong similarities between the relative number of firms in the different industries across the countries and that relative firm size is also similar between industries, although this feature was less marked. These produce a close association between concentration among the six, though do not appear 'to fully explain the coincidence in industry concentration'.[2]

The second of these is the study by Phlips (1971) which began as a comparative analysis of industrial structure in the EEC but ended up largely as an examination of certain relationships between concentration and other variables, such as R and D, price and wage rates, for the few countries (just Belgium in some cases) for which the necessary information was available. The main reason for this change in plan is given as the high incidence of gaps in the German size distribution figures. Indeed Phlips makes no attempt to overcome this problem and seems to us to bow much too readily before it, in view of our own experience in circumventing the intentions of the German authorities concerned to a reasonably satisfactory extent. Nevertheless

---

1   It may be worth noting also that in at least four of the 12 industries – steel, petrol refining, cement and brewing – costs were found still to be falling even at the scale of the largest plant actually in operation, and in these cases the size of the largest existing plant was taken as the measure of minimum optimal scale.

2   In order to fill in the gaps in the frequency distributions published for Germany, Horowitz assumed that the mean employment size of the firms included in any size class for which the total employment figure was withheld was equal to the average for that size class in the rest of the EEC countries, which might well give misleading results especially at the top end of the scale.

a comparison is made of the concentration ratios and plant size in the remaining five countries, from which an inverse relationship between concentration and domestic market size and a positive relationship between the latter and plant size emerges. Phlips makes a somewhat debatable attempt to allow for inter-country differences in relative market size by relating concentration ratios in each country to the number of enterprises in the particular industry and to their average employment size, which follows the procedure adopted by Pashigian in comparing the US and Britain. However, the r^2s obtained do not really seem high enough to justify this method of analysis, and the conclusions drawn — that, for instance, France has a relatively high degree of concentration after allowing for her generally greater market size — have to remain rather tentative. The more direct approach of relating ratios of persons engaged by the industry in question seems to represent a more satisfactory starting point.[1]

The main findings of these studies in comparative industrial structure may be summarised as follows:

A. *Concentration*
  (1) There is a general tendency for concentration to be inversely related to the size of the domestic market.
  (2) Concentration tends to be positively related to plant size especially in Western European countries.
  (3) The ranking of industries by concentration level tends to be similar in a number of countries.
  (4) There is also a similarity in the level of concentration in particular industries in several countries, but with the UK apparently being something of an exception, though the data used are not very satisfactory in this instance.

B. *Plants*
  (1) There is a positive association between plant size and market size.
  (2) The relative size ranking of average plant size across industries is similar as between countries.

C. *Firms*
  (1) There is a similarity in relative firm sizes across industries in EEC countries.
  (2) There is also a similarity in the relative number of firms across industries in EEC countries.

Our own analysis of the 1963 data represents an attempt to compare some aspects of industrial structure in the UK, Germany, France and Italy, with the objects of seeing: first, what differences exist in concentration and plant size between the largest four Western European countries; secondly, whether the findings of previous studies as to the similarity of concentration ratios and plant size in particular industries are confirmed; and thirdly, to examine further the relationship between industry size, plant size and concentration.

---

1   Pashigian uses this method as well as that noted above, but retains the ratios of average sizes of enterprise in the regression.

2. **The data**

(a) *1963 Census of Production comparisons*

The 1963 industrial enquiry carried out in each of the six EEC member countries provides a unique opportunity for examining industrial structure on a comparative basis, since, with minor exceptions, statistics were compiled according to a common industrial classification – la Nomenclature des Industries établies dans les Communautés Européennes (NICE). The pitfalls which inevitably surround such an exercise when national census material is used are therefore not present to anywhere near the same extent. Certain problems do remain, but are likely to be relatively minor. Those worth mentioning arise partly from the fact that the national authorities were each responsible for collecting their own figures; these relate to slightly different time periods, – for Germany to the end of September 1962[1] for France to January 1963 and for Italy to 16 October 1961 – and they are almost bound to vary in their coverage of the very small businesses – one-man concerns in particular.

A further problem concerns the high incidence of 'gaps' in the German data on the size distributions of enterprises and establishments, which are the source of our estimates of concentration ratios and employment sizes of the larger units. The official explanation for these omissions is that they are necessary in order to prevent the disclosure of information relating to individual businesses. However, this justification does not stand up to even cursory inspection, the omissions seemingly assuming a purely random character in a large number of instances. It is even true in some cases that the employment figure for only one size class is withheld, but as total persons engaged are given, the missing figure is readily found by a process of subtraction. A cynic might be tempted to ascribe the omissions to sheer bloody-mindedness on the part of the German authorities concerned, the effect being much more to extend the amount of time and effort needed to make reasonable estimates of the variables required than to prevent their calculation at all. Thus it is only in a very small number of instances that worthwhile comparisons with other countries are rendered impossible.

Much more serious difficulties arise of course when an attempt is made to compare the industrial structure of the continental countries with that of the UK, because of differences in the industrial classification adopted by the 1963 Census of Production. Nevertheless while comparisons cannot be made for all industries within the manufacturing sector, a reasonable degree of comparability can be attained for between 40 and 50 trades, in the sense that they seem to cover broadly similar activities – although it is impossible to be completely certain of this owing to the limited amount of information given. It should be said that in a number of cases, two or more census industries have been combined on one side in order to match the classification adopted by the other side. This applies more to the UK than to the EEC countries, as is to be expected in view of the greater number of 'industries' designated by the UK Census of Production; for example, 'Clothing' manufacture is covered by one 'NICE industry' but is divided into 8 industries by the UK Census for 1963. On the other side, the UK 'Scientific, Surgical and Photographic Instruments, etc.' covers three EEC industries.

---

1   While data on the number of establishments and enterprises were collected at this time, data on employment relate to the average figure during 1962.

In addition to classification difficulties, the EEC enquiry seems to have achieved a greater coverage of the very small businesses than the UK Census. To take West Germany as an example, the enquiry reports that a total of 1006 thousand were employed in manufacturing enterprises with a work force of less than ten people, as opposed to 165 thousand in the UK.[1] However, inspection of the size distributions for individual industries reveals that these very small businesses were concentrated in a very few activities in Germany, many of which are excluded althogether from the UK Census. This is illustrated in Table 2.1 which lists the most important areas of difference and compares the numbers engaged in enterprises employing less than ten people (in the UK ten or less) in these activities in the two countries.

Table 2.1 *Comparison of very small enterprises in UK and West Germany, 1962/63*

Industry	Number of enterprises employing less than 10 people[a]		Number of persons engaged in such enterprises ('000)[a]	
	Germany	UK	Germany	UK
Meat slaughtering and processing	33628	not included	136.5	not included
Bread and related products	40512	444	154.4	2.0
Shoe repair	32751	not included	47.5	not included
Clothing	64799	1781	108.3	10.1
Timber	36484	1018	106.6	5.7
Furniture	22674	924	58.3	5.2
Metal products	39080	4480	107.0	22.5
Motor vihicle and cycle repair	12137	not included	41.6	not included
Precision and optical instruments	5730	736	19.6	3.5
Watches and clocks[b]	2463	22	4.5	0.1
Total of above industries	290258	9405	784.2	49.1
Total all manufacturing	366106	30831	1006.2	165.0

Source: Office Statistique des Communautés Européennes, *Études et enquetês statistiques*, 2, 1969, Table F; Board of Trade, *Report on the Census of Production* 1963, HMSO, 1969.

Notes: [a] The size class in the case of the UK is 1–10 persons engaged, in the case of Germany 1–9. In addition, the UK figures relate to establishments rather than enterprises, but the two should be identical for this size of business.

[b] Includes repairing for Germany.

It is clear that these ten trades account for much the greater part of the overall disparity between the two countries as far as the reporting of these very small businesses is concerned. However, its effect on the subsequent analysis is relatively small, insofar as three of the trades are not included in the UK Census and for a fourth, 'Metal Products', it has proved impossible to reconcile classification differences, so that inter-country comparisons cannot be made. For the remaining six, the question

1 The relevant size class is 1–10 in the UK as against 1–9 in Germany, so that the difference is even greater than indicated.

11

of whether to include or exclude these businesses in the denominator of the concentration ratio calculations is not all that important, as either course of action in fact makes very little *absolute* difference to the results and, with the exception of 'Timber', does not alter the relative ranking of the two countries. In the case of 'Timber', omitting units employing less than ten people, raises the four-firm concentration ratio for Germany from 4 per cent to 8 per cent, the UK ratio remaining at 6 per cent. Since it is not unlikely that there are many more small businesses in this particular industry in Germany than in the UK we have assumed that the difference between the two census figures for total employment reflects the actual situation and have left the German ratio as 4 per cent.

Two further difficulties concern the definitions of the basic terms 'establishment' and 'enterprise'. The EEC enquiry adopts the term 'unité locale' as the basis for the compilation of what in the UK would be 'establishment' figures. The former covers the whole of a premises under common ownership at a particular location or site, which in fact is what the term establishment usually refers to in the UK Census. However, in a few cases when more than one activity is performed at the site and when separate accounting figures are kept for the individual activities, the UK Census, unlike the EEC enquiry, then counts each department or plant carrying out the different activities as one establishment and enters it into the appropriate Census industry. Allocation to industries is determined both in the UK and EEC by the principal products or product groups produced, or where a number of different products are manufactured, by the category which accounts for the greater part of output. It therefore follows that there will be more establishments recorded in the UK Census than 'unités locales' recorded in the EEC enquiry according to the number of premises which can be divided into more than one 'establishment' by the UK authorities, or according to the prevalence of the location of plants producing different products on the same site. There is no way of knowing how important this feature is in the UK or, in other words, how many fewer 'unités locales' than 'establishments' there would be in individual Census industries. We can only guess, and indeed hope, that the difference is not all that great, but nevertheless it may represent a serious qualification to a comparative analysis of plant size.

The second problem concerns an important difference in procedure between the two enquiries. Throughout the UK Census, the establishment is used as the basis for compilation: figures for enterprises are derived by aggregating those establishments under common ownership. If an enterprise owned establishments classified to different industries, then it too will appear in more than one industry. In contrast, the EEC enquiry collected separate figures for enterprises as distinct from those for 'unités locales'. In the same way as the latter, these were classified to industries on the basis of the product group produced or that representing the greater part of output. Each enterprise could therefore appear in only one industry, irrespective of the number of activities performed at separate plants. Because of this, there is no necessary reason why the enterprise figures for employment should correspond with the establishment figures. The two sets of figures would only be the same if each enterprise confined its activities to one industry, and the greater the extent of product diversification and multi-plant operations, the wider the divergence between the two. As compared with the UK practice, this procedure gives rise to a far greater possibility that some important producers will not be included in the enterprise figures for a particular industry or that a significant proportion of the work-force will be engaged in manufacturing 'other' products. There is no straightforward way of overcoming this problem and we have evaded it by including in our comparisons of enterprise concentration ratios involving the UK only those industries for which the EEC enquiry gives broadly similar employment totals for both enterprises and 'unités locales'. For the comparisons of the three mainland European countries, all industries for which data are available or can be satisfactorily estimated, have been included, and any interpretation of the results should recognise the possibility that variations in the extent of product diversification might be of some importance in particular cases, though the indications are that these are relatively few in number.

(b) *Method of estimating concentration ratios and average sizes of firm and plant from size distributions*

There are a number of alternative variables which can be used as a basis for comparing concentration and the size of plants or enterprises. Sales, net output, net assets and employment are the four most frequently used. The relative merits of one as against the others depend very much on the specific issue at hand. In our case, however, we are obliged to express comparisons in terms of employment as this is the only measure available; whether another variable would be more satisfactory is therefore academic. While various studies have shown that there is a tendency for different measures of concentration to produce similar results,[1] these have generally been concerned with inter-industry comparisons within a single country rather than between countries, and there is really no way of knowing how our findings would be altered by the use of an alternative measure. It is as well to bear in mind that there are apparent differences in the level of output per person engaged as between countries and that these do not appear to be uniform as between industries. This implies that different results might emerge if sales or net output rather than employment were used as the basis for comparison. For example, the generally higher level of labour productivity in Germany *vis à vis* the UK means that the relative size of German units in terms of output tends to be greater than indicated by employment comparisons.

Given the necessity of using employment as an indicator of size, there remains the question of deriving comparative figures from the size distributions of plants and enterprises published in the relevant censuses. We have conducted the analysis largely in terms of the largest four enterprises and the largest 20 plants in each industry in the different countries, and in order to estimate the average sizes of these and their percentage share of employment from the published frequency distributions, we have used the conventional method developed by Bain (1966, pp 26–29). This involves calculating minimum and maximum values for the average size or percentage share of the largest units, and taking the arithmetic mean of the two. If, for example, the Census shows that, in a particular industry, the largest six firms belonged to the size class 5,000 or more and had a total labour force of 42,000, the minimum number employed by the largest four would be 4 × 7000 – assuming the six were all of equal size – and the maximum number would be 42,000 minus

---

1 See, for example, Sawyer (1971).

(2 × 5000) (5,000 being the lower limit of the size class). For this industry, therefore, we would estimate that 30,000 (the arithmetic mean of 28,000 and 32,000) were employed by the largest four enterprises. In the case of Germany, where necessary, we have followed a similar procedure to estimate the figures omitted for 'disclosure reasons'; that is, we have calculated minimum and maximum values for such figures and incorporated each of these in the estimation of the numbers employed by the largest four or 20 units.

It has only been necessary to calculate the estimates referred to above for the UK and Germany, as a similar exercise has been performed by Phlips for France and Italy, using the same method of estimation. It should be said, however, that there are certain qualifications surrounding the use of Phlips' figures; in particular, the average size of plant or firm is not derived directly from the frequency distributions but from the estimated concentration ratios. In other words, for some reason he has adopted the procedure of multiplying total employment by the already estimated concentration ratio in order to obtain the number engaged in the relevant number of largest units. This would be unexceptional were it not for the fact that concentration ratios rounded to whole numbers have been used in the calculation, which, of course, means that the answers are liable to differ to varying degrees from the 'direct' estimates, the difference increasing with the size of the industry.[1] Nevertheless we have not considered this qualification sufficiently important to justify the rather tedious recomputation of the French and Italian figures, although in a few cases where Phlips' averages are misleading, we have recalculated them directly from the frequency distributions.

For the UK and Germany, we found in the majority of cases that the difference between the minimum and maximum estimates was not particularly significant, in the sense that the inclusion of one rather than the other in the analysis would alter the results only marginally. For a few industries, however, the spread is very wide and an average of the two extremes might be very different from the actual value. Where this is so, we have omitted the industry concerned from the analysis. (This usually applies to Germany because of the withholding of figures from the size distributions.) Phlips unfortunately does not give the margin of error for the French and Italian industry estimates.

---

1 It also produces some slightly strange results where the average size of the largest 4 and the largest 8 firms are being compared and where concentration ratios are very small. If, for example, the 4-firm ratio is one per cent and the 8-firm ratio two per cent, then, of course, Phlips' procedure leads to the average size of the largest 8 firms being identical with that of the largest 4.

3
Concentration and the size of enterprises

As outlined in the chapter dealing with previous research work, increasing attention in this field is being devoted to international comparisons of concentration, of the size of plants and enterprises, and of the interrelationships between them. This chapter examines comparative concentration levels and enterprise sizes in four EEC countries. Analysis of the size of plant is left until the next chapter.

1. Concentration ratios

A common finding in international comparisons of industrial concentration is the similarity in the pattern of concentration in terms of levels, and especially in terms of the ranking of industries. Why should this be so? First, it should be noted that empirical analysis of cost curves shows that there is typically a wide range of approximately constant costs, so that a wide range of concentration ratios would be compatible in most industries with firms operating at minimum costs. On technical grounds, therefore, it is difficult to see any reason why concentration ratios should tend towards uniformity for particular industries in different economies, even if those economies were broadly similar in size. Technical factors will, however, dictate differences in minimum optimal scales between industries, and will therefore explain a broad similarity in the ranking of industries by the level of concentration. But because of differences in the minimum optimal size of firm in relation to the size of the market, together with the tendency towards constant costs, these broad similarities need not bring about similar concentration levels within industries in different countries.

One explanation for the emergence of similar concentration levels for individual industries in different countries is that market structures tend to evolve until they become acceptable to firms in terms of profit and the uncertainties of competition. For each industry there will, for given technological and market conditions, be a limit to the amount of competition which firms are ready to accept. P.W.S. Andrews (1964) summed this up when referring to the equilibrium of the firm with its environment. "We can still retain ideas of a firm in balance, a sort of equilibrium; but this would be a balance with its environment, the industrial environment." Firms, therefore, are likely to seek a restriction of competition to the extent necessary to yield an acceptable or normal return on capital. Patterns of market structure and business conduct which do not result in orderly competition and acceptable returns will be unstable and will result in fundamental change.

But whether or not this is a strong unifying factor depends on how firms perceive their environment. If they are influenced essentially by domestic competitive pressures then there seems no reason to expect that very similar market structures would emerge. After all there are major differences between countries in such factors as monopoly legislation, the rate of growth of markets, financial institutions, and innate propensities to compete, which would lead to different 'equilibrium' structures in different economies. On the other hand, the greater the influence on industries in different countries of international competitive forces, the greater is the tendency towards uniformity in concentration levels likely to be. And where the nature of the product is such as to give rise to serious dangers of price wars, internal as well as external pressures towards high concentration will be strong.

If we turn to the results of comparing concentration across the four countries which are the concern of this study, these by and large confirm the findings of other investigators in this area. In particular, there is a broad similarity in the rank order of industries by concentration ratio as between the UK, West Germany, France and Italy. This can be seen from Table 3.1 which presents the results of regressing the four-firm employment concentration ratios shown by the industries in one country on those of another for each pair of countries. The correlation coefficients are all significantly positive indicating that the highly concentrated trades in any one of the countries also tend to be highly concentrated trades in the other three.

Table 3.1 *Regression equations of 4-firm employment concentration ratios in pairs of countries, 1963*

Regression equation	Constant		Regression coefficient	Correlation coefficient	Number of industries
UK on Germany	16.9 (5.0)	+	0.871 (0.205)	0.56	41
UK on France	17.3 (3.8)	+	0.728 (0.123)	0.69	41
UK on Italy	17.1 (3.5)	+	0.672 (0.102)	0.73	41
Germany on France	8.1 (2.3)	+	0.514 (0.073)	0.75	41
Germany on France	6.6 (1.8)	+	0.659 (0.053)	0.80	90
Germany on Italy	9.7 (2.0)	+	0.561 (0.059)	0.71	90
France on Italy	7.6 (2.2)	+	0.739 (0.065)	0.77	90

Note: The regression equation in each case is $C_i^j = a + bC_i^k$, where C_i^j and C_i^k are the 4-firm employment concentration ratios in the ith industry in country j and country k, respectively.

Considering the regression equations involving the UK, the relative size of the regression coefficients indicate, given the similarity of the constant terms, that British industries tend to be more concentrated *vis à vis* their counterparts in Germany than is the case as compared with industries in France or Italy. What is not immediately clear from Table 3.1, however, is that British industries tend to show a substantially higher degree of concentration than the same industries in the other three countries.

Table 3.2 *Employment-weighted average 4-firm concentration ratios: 41 industries and all manufacturing, 1963*

	UK	Germany	France	Italy
Weighted average, 41 industries	30	19	22	19
Weighted average, 'all manufacturing'	32	22	24	20

Notes: The 'all-manufacturing' weighted average concentration ratios do not in fact cover the entire manufacturing sectors of each country, but in the case of Germany, France and Italy are based on 90 EEC census industries. In the case of the UK the ratio is taken from Sawyer (1971).

A general impression of the overall level of concentration is given in Tables 3.2 and 3.3. The former gives the weighted average concentration ratios for the four countries, using the numbers employed in the respective industries as weights, over the trades for which a comparison is possible. Thus whereas the largest four enterprises in any industry in Germany, France or Italy accounted, on average, for around 20 per cent of employment, in the UK the comparable figure is 30 per cent. This result is little altered if a comparison is made on the basis of all census trades for which the necessary details are published. It would appear therefore that the 41 industries included in the study are fairly representative of the manufacturing sector as a whole in all four countries at least as far as concentration is concerned.

Further analysis of the UK-West German comparison is given in Table 3.3. in which the 41 industries are grouped in terms of the 4-firm concentration ratio in the UK. The table not only demonstrates once more the essential similarity in industry ranking by concentration, but that the biggest disparity in the level of concentration between the two countries tends to occur in those industries which are highly concentrated in the UK. Thus the average concentration ratio calculated for Group A is over twice as high in this country as compared with the average for the same industries in Germany, whereas in the case of Group D there is very little difference.

Table 3.3 *Average 4-firm concentration ratios: 41 industries in the UK and West Germany, 1963*

Industry group	UK	West Germany
A (11)	62	28
B (10)	39	24
C (10)	22	16
D (10)	13	12
Weighted average (41 industries)	30	19

Notes: The 41 industries are arranged in descending order of their concentration ratio in the UK and divided into groups of 10 or 11.

A more detailed analysis of the comparison of concentration levels in the UK and other EEC countries is given in the scatter diagrams — Figures 3.1 to 3.3. Figure 3.1 for example shows that in all but five of the 41 industries concentration was higher in the UK than in Germany. Similarly, though the pattern is not quite as extreme, Figures 3.2 and 3.3 show that only ten French industries and eleven Italian ones were more highly concentrated than comparable British industries. The observations which lie furthest above the 45 degree line and all those which lie below have been noted on the diagrams. Considering these, it is apparent that the food and drink trades are well represented in the former group, while there is

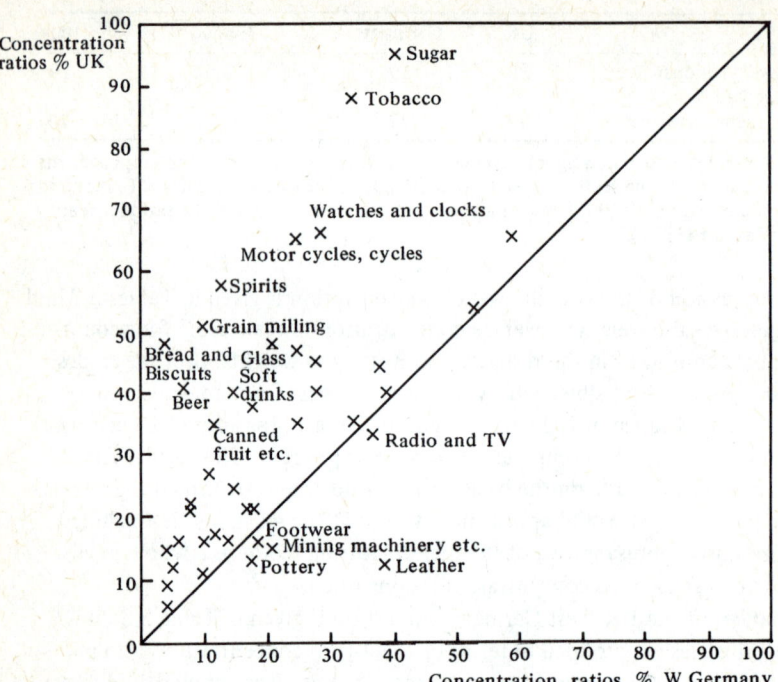

Fig. 3.1 *4-Firm employment concentration ratios, 41 industries, UK/Germany*

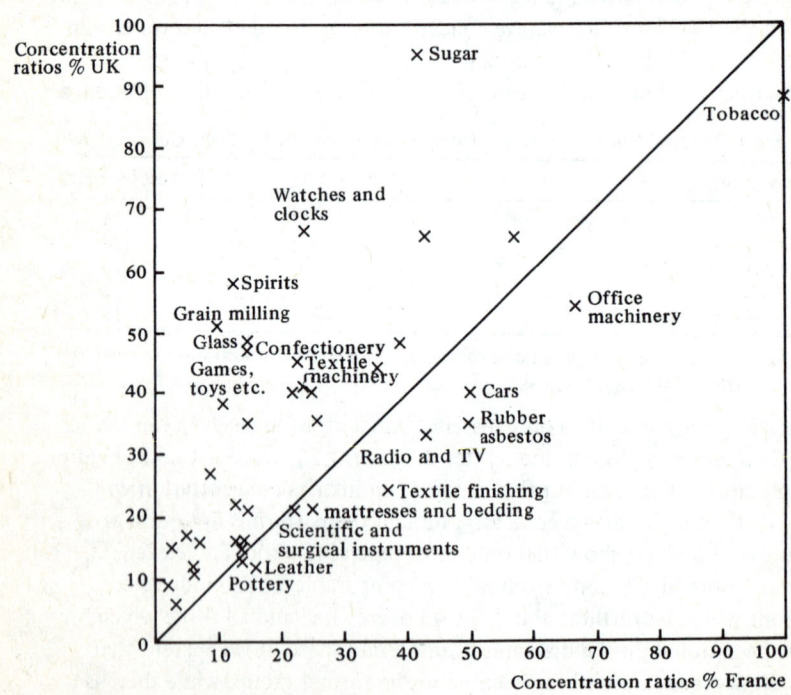

Fig. 3.2 *4-Firm employment concentration ratios, 41 industries, UK/France*

Fig. 3.3 *4-Firm employment concentration ratios, 41 industries, UK/Italy*

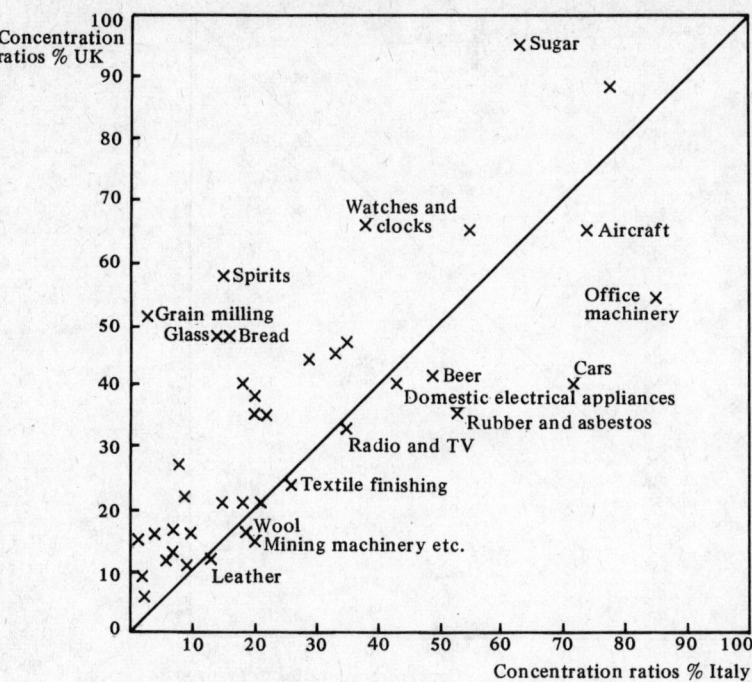

Fig. 3.4 *4-Firm employment concentration ratios, 41 industries, Germany/France*

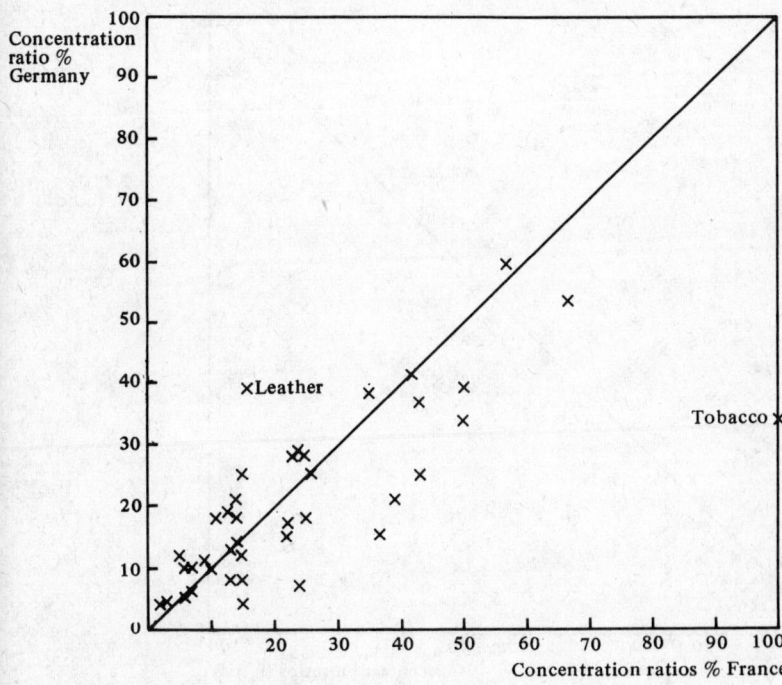

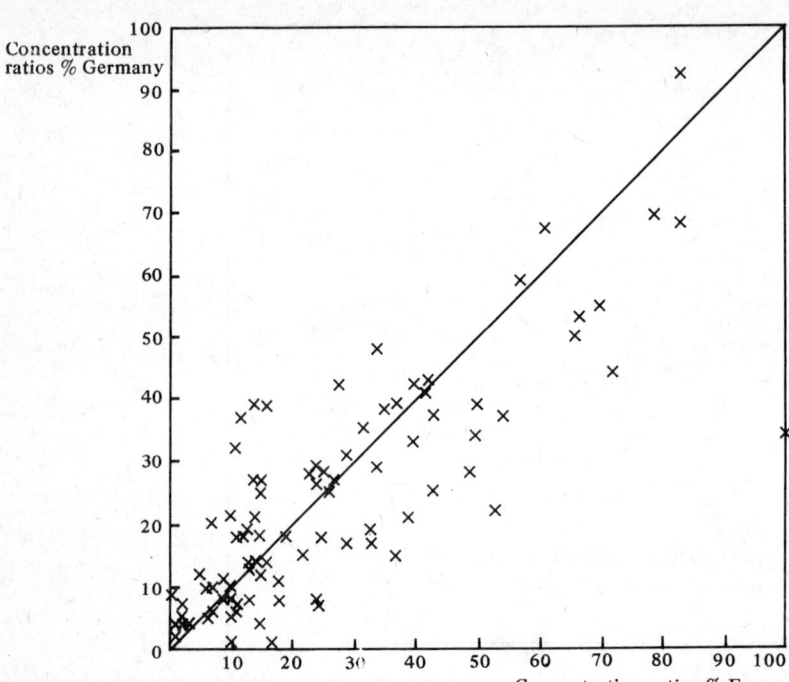

Fig. 3.5 *4-Firm employment concentration ratios, 90 industries, Germany/France*

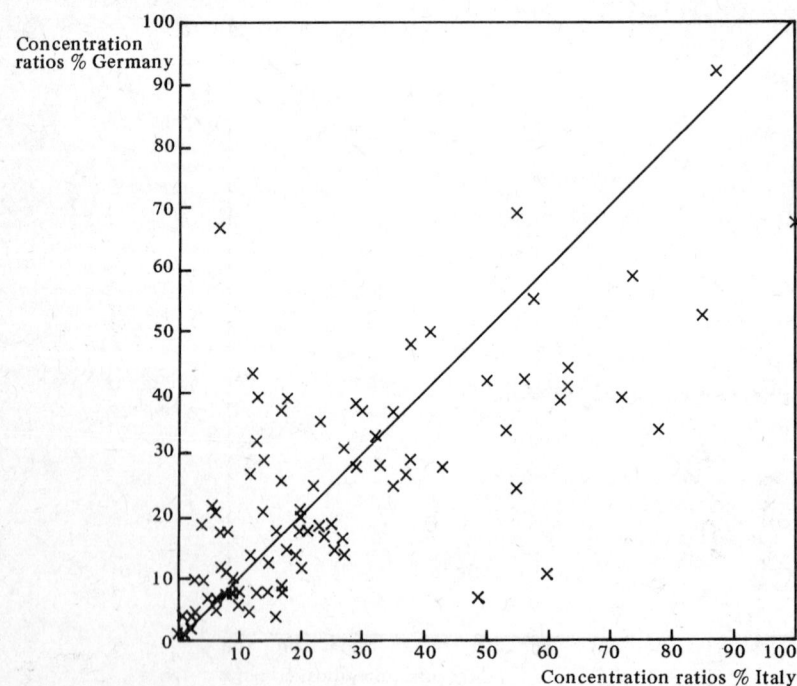

Fig. 3.6 *4-Firm employment concentration ratios, 90 industries, Germany/Italy*

Fig. 3.7 *4-Firm employment concentration ratios, 90 industries, France/Italy*

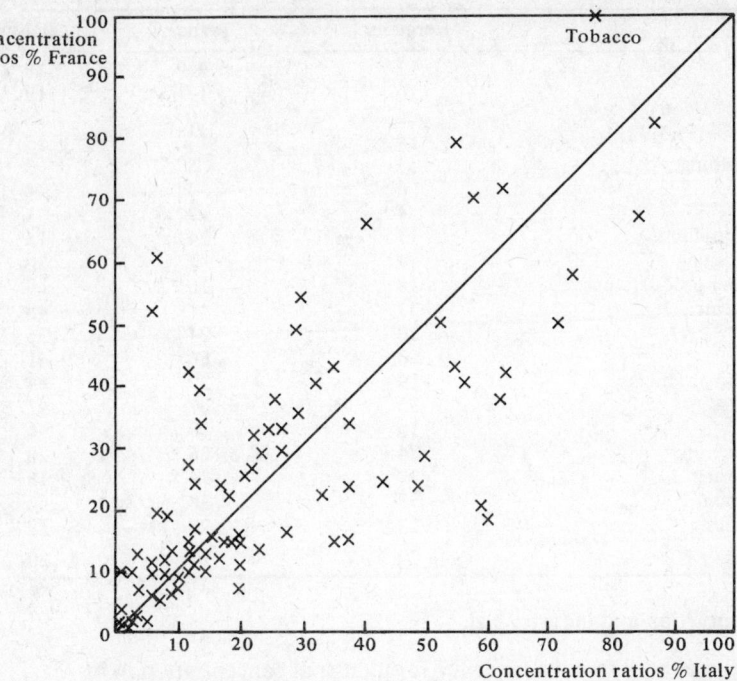

some similarity in the trades which have comparatively low concentration ratios in the UK. This is so, in particular, as regards the comparisons with France and Italy, six of the industries below the line being the same in both cases – these are office machinery, cars, textile finishing, leather, radio and TV, and rubber and asbestos.

While the UK seems, in general, to have a higher level of concentration than the other countries a comparison of concentration levels in Germany, France and Italy suggests a great deal of similarity. Thus in Table 3.4 a striking similarity in concentration ratios is shown for most industries. Tobacco, which in France is under state ownership, and electrical engineering where concentration in Italy is far lower than in Germany and France, are the only industries where a big difference in concentration exists. Similarly, in contrast to Figures 3.1 to 3.3, the general picture shown in Figures 3.4 to 3.7 shows a much more even scatter of observations around the 45 degree line, indicating a greater similarity in the average degree of industrial concentration.

Even allowing for measurement errors in making international comparisions of industrial structure there can be little doubt that major differences exist between the UK and other West European countries of similar size, and that these appear to be much greater than those existing between the older members of the EEC. Part of the explanation for this is likely to be found in the different competitive environment in which UK firms have been operating in terms of such factors as the rate of growth of markets, the ability to engage in collusive behaviour and the financial links between companies.

Table 3.4 *Employment weighted 4-firm concentration ratios: 20 two-digit industries, Germany, France and Italy, 1963*

Industry group	Germany	France	Italy
Food	12	20	18
Drink	10	17	19
Tobacco	34	100	78
Textiles	14	17	15
Footwear and clothing	7	5	3
Wood-working	6	4	4
Wood-furniture	4	3	1
Paper and paper products	17	14	15
Printing and publishing	4	7	10
Leather and leather products	18	10	9
Rubber, asbestos, etc.	32	46	48
Chemicals	30	24	35
Petroleum	50	66	41
Other non-metallic products	19	29	14
Metals	35	37	41
Metal products	10	9	4
Mechanical engineering	24	26	28
Electrical engineering	39	44	18
Transport equipment	33	38	46
Other manufactures	23	20	19
All manufacturing	22	24	20

2 Concentration and industry size

A number of studies have found a tendency for industrial concentration to be negatively associated with the relative size of individual industries, which some investigators have taken as a proxy for market size – effectively ignoring the difference that international trade can make to the one relative to the other. Such a tendency is just about evident in the inter-country comparisons made here, but not in those involving the UK. Comparing the UK with West Germany, for instance, out of 41 industries the concentration ratio is higher in the UK in 36 cases. Of these, the size of industry in terms of employment is larger in the UK in 14 instances and in Germany in the remaining 22. And the five industries in which concentration is higher in Germany are also larger in Germany than in the UK. In 22 out of 41 industries therefore there is a negative association between the concentration ratio and the size of the industry, but in the remaining 19 cases the association is a positive one.

To examine this relationship further we have taken the ratio of the four-firm concentration ratios in each industry as between each pair of countries and regressed this on the ratio of industry size. The regression equations are shown in Table 3.5.[1] Those involving the UK bear out what was said above, the regression coefficients clearly being not significantly different from zero, indicating no tendency for concentration to increase as the size of industry in the UK declines relative to either Germany or France. In the case of the equations not involving the UK however a slight negative association between the variables is evident, though the regression coefficients are not in all cases significant at the five per cent level.

1   In this and the following tables we have not included the UK-Italy comparisons, first because there are a number of industries which are overwhelmingly bigger in the UK, and secondly because in the remaining cases the Italian pattern is very similar to that of France.

Table 3.5 *Regression equations of concentration on industry size, pairs of countries, 1963*

Regression equation[a]	Constant		Regression coefficient	Correlation coefficient	Number of industries
UK : W. Germany	2.4	—	0.116 (0.227)	0.08	41
UK : France	2.0	—	0.000 (0.163)	0.00	41
Germany : France	1.3	—	0.094 (0.056)	0.26	41
Germany : France	1.4	—	0.086 (0.036)	0.26	83[b]
Germany : Italy	1.7	—	0.106 (0.053)	0.22	83[b]
France : Italy	1.6	—	0.134 (0.093)	0.16	83[b]

[a] The equations relate the ratios of concentration ratios – the dependent variable, to the ratios of industry size – the independent variable.

[b] Industries which vary enormously in size (by 20 times or more) have been excluded, as has Tobacco which is a state monopoly in France.

3 The average size of the largest enterprises

In addition to examining concentration ratios attention has also been focused directly on the size of the largest four enterprises in each industry in the four countries, in order to see whether the results of the concentration comparisons are confirmed. Thus while care has been taken to match the UK industries with the appropriate German, French and Italian trades, there is no way of knowing how important the differences in coverage, which must inevitably remain, in fact are. As such differences are more likely to affect the denominator of the concentration measure than the numerator, an examination of the latter on its own provides a useful check to the conclusions reached above.

Looking at the UK comparisons, it is clear that these tend to conform to what we would expect to find on the basis of the concentration ratio findings. The details are show in Appendix 3.1. UK firms are larger than German ones in 29 out of 41 industries, larger than French ones in 37 industries and larger than Italian ones in all but one industry. For the 41 industries the leading UK firms are on average 2.2 times as large as their German counterparts and 3.5 times as large as leading French firms.

4 The size of firms and industries

In order to see how the size of the largest firms varies with size of industry we have followed the same procedure as above. As in the case of concentration ratios we have taken the ratios of these two variables as between each pair of countries as a measure of relative size. The results of the regression analysis for pairs of countries are shown in Table 3.6. They show that there is a very definite positive relationship between firm size and industry size, but also that while relative industry size is a contributory factor influencing differences in firm size between countries, it is by no means the only factor which underlies such differences.

Table 3.6 *Regression equations of firm size on industry size, pairs of countries, 1963*

Regression equation[a]	Constant		Regression coefficient	Correlation coefficient	Number of industries
UK on Germany	1.0	+	1.111 (0.206)	0.65	41
UK on France	−1.1	+	2.596 (0.292)	0.82	41
Germany on France	0.7	+	0.704 (0.066)	0.76	83[b]
Germany on Italy	1.2	+	0.729 (0.111)	0.59	83[b]
France on Italy	0.7	+	0.753 (0.085)	0.70	83[b]

[a] The equations relate the ratios of firm size – the dependent variable, to the ratios of industry size – the independent variable.

[b] Excluding Tobacco, in which France has a state monopoly, and six industries where there are very large differences in industry size between two or all four of the countries.

Looking at the UK–German comparison in more detail, it is a striking feature of Appendix 3.1 that all the 12 industries in which the largest German firms were bigger than their British counterparts were also larger, in terms of employment, in Germany than in the UK. On the other hand it is clearly not the case that the British industries in which firms were larger than in Germany were necessarily those with a larger labour force. In 15 of the 29 industries with a larger firm size, the employment size of industry was in fact lower in the UK than in Germany, although most of these 15 were relatively larger in Britain than the 12 where firms were smaller than in Germany. Nevertheless, as is clear from Appendix 3.1, there are a number of industries where there is great difficulty in explaining the relative size of the largest British companies in terms of larger industry size. These include in particular bread, biscuits, etc., beer and spirits.

5   Concentration, firm size and industry size

Relating the size of firm and of industry to concentration it is found that in the five industries in which Germany has the higher concentration ratio it also has the larger firms as well as the larger industries. Thus with regard to these trades higher concentration in Germany results from the biggest enterprises being relatively larger than those in Britain, rather than from the employment size of industry being smaller.
Of the 36 industries in which the UK has the higher concentration ratio it also has the larger firms and the larger industries in 14 cases. For these also higher UK concentration is due to larger UK firms. In 7 cases higher UK concentration is combined with smaller firms and smaller industries so that here higher UK concentration is due to relatively small industry size. In the remaining 15 industries higher UK concentration is combined with larger firms and smaller industries so that both relative firm and relative industry size contribute towards the higher level of concentration. These various industry groups are identified in Appendix 3.2 of this chapter.

As regards the comparison between France and Germany, it is evident from Appendix 3.1 that Germany has the largest enterprises in all but a few trades.[1] As Germany is not, in general, more highly concentrated than France, this larger firm size is clearly coupled with greater industry size in the majority of instances.

6 Summary and interpretation of main conclusions

The main conclusions of this chapter may be summarised as follows:

(1) For all countries there is a tendency for relative concentration in different industries to be similar, i.e. the high concentration industries in one country tend to be the high concentration industries of another and *vice versa*. The relative concentration levels are more closely related to relative firm size than to relative industry size.

(2) There is a strong positive association between firm size and industry size, and there is limited evidence of a negative association between concentration and industry size. The latter, however, where it does exist, is rather weak. In particular the UK with an industrial labour force only slightly smaller than Germany's in 1963, but bigger than France's or Italy's emerges as by far the most highly concentrated of the four. Thus, while the hypothesis of a negative association may have some validity if a sufficently wide range of industry sizes are considered it does not seem to hold as a general proposition.

(3) The level of concentration is, in general, very similar in Germany, France and Italy, but in the UK concentration levels tend to be substantially higher.

There are a number of possible reasons as to why British industries are considerably more concentrated in general than their counterparts in the other three large West European countries. Detailed research is needed before any firm conclusions can be arrived at, and such research will form part of future work on the project. In the meantime we can speculate that certain features of the UK economy which differ from those of the other three countries might have played some role in bringing about the observed result.

First, the official attitude towards restrictive trade agreements between companies has been much tougher in the UK than in the other countries. As a result of the 1956 Restrictive Trade Practices Act British firms were forced to abandon the more blatant forms of restrictions on trade. By 1963 more than half the agreements registered under the Act had been abandoned; a likely effect of this is that firms would seek other means to limit the effects of competition. The most obvious and certainly the surest way of achieving this is through mergers which may reduce the number of competing firms and increase the market share of the leaders. One would certainly not expect the structural consequences of the 1956 Act to have worked themselves out completely by 1963 but their impact had probably been more than trivial by that date. In Germany, France and Italy, by contrast, a stronger tradition of cartelisation has continued and certainly anti-trust legislation in the 1950's and early 1960's

---

[1] The French tobacco industry should really be excluded from the comparison because it is a state monopoly, while in view of the limitations placed on German aircraft production, the same applies to the aircraft industry.

was either almost non-existent or largely ineffective, a reflection of the greater willingness on the part of the authorities to contemplate price-fixing or market-sharing agreements between firms. On this score therefore the incentive to merge was less than in the UK.

Secondly, the finance of industry has differed in important respects in the UK from the general pattern in the other three countries. In particular, the banking system in the latter has traditionally played a considerably more significant role in providing finance for investment than is the case in the UK. Such a system, especially where there are only a small number of large commercial banks, as in Germany, can clearly represent a means of ensuring that the common interests of superficially independent companies are pursued as well as providing a meeting ground for the exchange of information. Moreover this type of financial arrangement is likely to place a lower premium on the absolute size of a company as a determinant of the allocation of investment funds, than in the British system in which the Stock Market and share valuation exert a major influence. Indeed one important motive for merger is to gain access to finance, and the incentive to merge from this standpoint has again been stronger in the UK than in the other countries.

Thirdly, the fact that the UK market has expanded much less quickly than has been the case in the older EEC countries may also have contributed towards a higher level of concentration. Where expansion is slow there may well be a greater tendency for firms to look towards external expansion by acquisition or merger rather than to internal expansion because of the greater safety which it affords the firm. More specifically the slower the growth of markets the greater the likelihood, other things being equal, that competitive investment plans will lead to the emergence of excess capacity. Mergers and a higher level of concentration may be 'necessary' in a slow growing market therefore to give businessmen the required degree of safety from the danger of price cutting activity.

In summary then factors such as differences in patterns of business conduct, sources of finance and rate of market expansion may have required a higher level of concentration in the UK than in the other countries.

Appendix 3.1 *Ratios of industry size and of the average size of the 4 largest firms, UK, Germany, and France, 41 industries, 1963*

Industry	Firm size UK : Germany	Firm size UK : France	Firm size Germany France	Industry size UK : Germany	Industry size UK : France	Industry size Germany France
Canned fruit and veg.	7.51	6.71	0.89	2.52	2.85	1.13
Grain milling	6.04	5.53	0.92	1.23	1.08	0.88
Bread, biscuits, etc.	9.71	22.40	2.31	0.85	7.05	8.31
Sugar	2.45	1.43	0.58	1.05	0.63	0.60
Confectionery	3.17	11.19	3.53	1.67	3.54	2.13
Alcohol, liquors	3.27	2.79	0.85	0.76	0.63	0.83
Beer and malt	5.28	7.01	1.33	0.86	4.10	4.76
Soft drinks	2.67	6.03	2.26	1.03	3.34	3.23
Tobacco	1.97	0.59	0.30	0.82	2.91	3.55
Wool	2.20	1.84	0.84	1.95	1.66	0.85
Hosiery	1.33	2.95	2.22	0.84	1.33	1.58
Textile finishing	2.47	1.09	0.44	1.55	1.65	1.06
Footwear	0.80	1.36	1.69	0.97	1.13	1.16
Clothing	1.62	5.98	3.69	0.81	1.36	1.68
Mattresses and bedding	1.14	1.31	1.15	0.97	1.57	1.62
Fur goods	1.39	1.96	1.40	0.55	0.95	1.71
Timber	0.47	0.65	1.40	0.34	0.33	0.98
Wood furniture	1.65	5.42	3.29	0.44	1.12	2.80
Paper and board	1.50	2.23	1.49	1.07	1.64	1.54
Paper and board products	1.65	6.47	3.92	1.20	1.96	1.63
Printing and publishing	3.28	4.55	1.39	1.32	1.99	1.51
Leather – tanning and dressing	0.23	0.91	3.93	0.79	1.25	1.60
Leather products	0.79	1.03	1.29	0.35	0.53	1.50
Rubber and asbestos	1.17	1.09	0.93	1.14	1.57	1.37
Plastic	0.78	2.72	3.48	0.74	1.58	2.14
General chemicals	0.48	1.43	2.95	0.42	1.11	2.61
Baked clay products and pottery	0.56	1.91	3.43	0.76	1.99	2.63
Glass	1.82	1.47	0.81	0.80	1.19	1.49
Office machinery	0.48	0.79	1.63	0.47	0.97	2.07
Metal working machine toos	1.22	1.89	1.55	0.42	1.10	2.59
Textile machinery	1.06	5.04	4.74	0.67	2.57	3.85
Mining, steel working machinery	0.33	1.67	5.12	0.45	1.56	3.49
Electronic apparatus etc.	0.58	1.90	3.25	0.66	2.48	3.77
Domestic electrical appliances	0.89	3.63	4.10	0.62	2.27	3.63
Automobiles and parts	1.03	1.08	1.05	1.01	1.34	1.33
Motorcycles and cycles	2.30	1.79	0.78	0.90	1.18	1.31
Aircraft	10.13	3.20	0.32	9.22	2.82	0.31
Scientific instruments	1.03	1.34	1.30	0.81	1.42	1.75
Watches and clocks	0.61	1.38	2.28	0.27	0.51	1.86
Jewellery, silverware	1.96	3.58	1.82	0.82	1.18	1.44
Games, toys, sports goods	2.42	4.65	1.92	1.17	1.34	1.15
Average 41 industries	2.23	3.46	2.01	0.93[a]	1.78	2.08

[a] Excluding aircraft

Appendix 3.2 *UK–West German industry comparisons*

Industries in which UK has :			
Higher concentration Larger firms Larger industries	Higher concentration Larger firms Smaller industries	Higher concentration Smaller firms Smaller industries	Lower concentration Smaller firms Smaller industries
Canned fruit and veg. Grain milling	Bread, biscuits Alcohol, liquors	Timber Leather products	Footwear Leather–tanning and dressing
Sugar	Beer and malt	Plastic	Pottery
Confectionery	Tobacco	General chemicals	Mining machinery
Soft drinks	Hosiery	Office machinery	Electronic apparatus
Wool	Clothing	Domestic electrical appliances	
Textile finishing	Mattresses and bedding	Watches and clocks	
Paper and board	Fur goods		
Paper and board products	Wood furniture		
Printing and publishing	Glass		
Automobiles and parts	Metal working machine tools		
Aircraft	Textile machinery		
Games, toys	Motor cycles and cycles		
Rubber and asbestos	Scientific instruments Jewellery, silverware		

4

Comparisons of plant size

We now turn our attention to manufacturing establishments rather than enterprises, taking the twenty largest plants in each industry as the main basis of comparison. The chapter is concerned with the following questions: first, how does the average size of UK plants compare to that of other European countries; secondly, how similar are plant concentration ratios for the same industry in different countries; thirdly, is there any systematic relationship between plant size and industry size and between plant concentration ratios and industry size; fourthly, how does the UK compare with West Germany in terms of the number of large plants (i.e. those employing 1000 or more) and in terms of changes over time in the size and number of such plants; and finally, is there any evidence in the UK or Germany that these large plants have a higher level of labour productivity than smaller ones?

1 Average plant size

Table 4.1 shows the average plant size for four countries, weighted by employment in each industry. As far as the UK is concerned perhaps the most relevant comparison to consider is that with West Germany, since the structure of industry in terms of the distribution of the labour force between the various activities is very similar in these two countries. Looking at the UK : Germany comparison, it is immediately apparent that the relative size of German plants *vis à vis* the UK is much greater than the relative size of German firms. Indeed in 24 of the 47 industries included in the comparison, German plants are larger in terms of employment than their British counterparts. In one industry plants are of equal size, and in the remaining 22, British plants are larger. Appendix 4.1 shows that German plant sizes are generally larger, often substantially so, in engineering, metals, and vehicles, clothing and paper products.

The divergence between the results of comparing plant size and comparing firm size may conceivably arise from the difference in the Census definition of establishment as between the UK and the EEC, in the sense that this tends to bias the findings in this particular direction. However, examination of the UK–France data shows that in only five out of 50 industries included in the analysis do French plants employ a larger labour force than British ones, which accords with the results of comparing firm sizes between these two countries – though strangely enough only one of the five trades also has larger firms in France than in the UK. It is, therefore, not obvious that differences in the definition of establishments as between the two countries act in a significantly biassed way in this case.

As far as Germany–France–Italy comparisons are concerned, Germany clearly

Table 4.1 *Weighted average size of the 20 largest plants, 1963*

Country	Number of industries	Average size[a] ('000 employees)
UK	47	3.13
Germany	47	3.73
France	47	2.09
Italy	47	0.99
UK	50	3.06
France	50	2.00
Italy	50	1.03
Germany	87	3.04
France	87	1.68
Italy	87	0.82

[a] Average number of persons engaged in the 20 largest plants weighted by employment in each industry.

Table 4.2 *Average size of the 20 largest plants by industry groups, UK, Germany, France and Italy*

Industry group[a]	Average size of plant ('000)			
	UK	Germany	France	Italy
A (10)	4.65	5.51	3.04	1.64
B (10)	1.92	1.80	0.79	0.77
C (9)	1.26	1.34	0.68	0.66
D (9)	0.73	0.72	0.43	0.41
E (9)	0.38	0.50	0.32	0.20

[a] The 47 industries are arranged in descending order of their size in the UK and divided into groups of 9 or 10.

tends to have considerably larger plants than either France or Italy, while French industries tend to have larger plants than their Italian counterparts. The details are shown in Appendix 4.1 to this chapter.

Not unexpectedly, there is a general tendency for industries which are characterised by relatively large plants in one country also to have relatively large plants in another, which suggests the influence of technical factors. The data are summarised in Table 4.2. Looking at the UK : Germany data, there is also a close correspondence in the average size of the largest plants for the various industry groups.

But although the rank-order of industries and average levels of plant size are similar as between the two countries there are important areas of difference as well. Thus if we look at the particular activities in which the UK has the relatively large plants we again find that the food, drink and tobacco trades bulk large, accounting for almost half the cases where the UK comes out ahead of Germany. In contrast in almost all the engineering industries, especially if Aircraft – which is subject to special circumstances – and cycles are excluded, the largest German plants are bigger – sometimes considerably so – than in Britain. Table 4.3 summarises the position with respect to the average size both of plant and of enterprise in 41 industries. In *all* trades where German firms are larger than British firms, German plants are also larger, whereas in only 19 of the 29 trades in which the UK has larger firms are British plants also larger than German ones. In the 19 industries in which the UK has both larger firms and larger plants, food, drink and tobacco trades are particularly well represented. In chemicals, metal products and engineering trades, however,

Table 4.3 *Relative size of largest enterprises and plants, UK and West Germany, 41 industries, 1963*

	Relative size of 20 largest plants		Relative size of 4 largest plants	
A. Industries in which UK firms > German firms	UK larger	German larger	UK larger	German larger
Canned frozen fruit & veg.	✓		✓	
Grain milling	✓		✓	
Bread, biscuits, etc.	✓		✓	
Sugar	✓		✓	
Confectionery	✓		✓	
Alcohol, yeast, liquors	✓		✓	
Beer & malt	✓		✓	
Soft drinks	✓		n.a.	
Tobacco	✓		✓	
Wool		n.a.		n.a.
Hosiery	✓		✓	
Textile finishing		✓		✓
Clothing	✓		✓	
Matresses & bedding	same size			✓
Fur goods	✓		✓	
Wood furniture		✓		✓
Paper & board	✓		✓	
Paper & board products	✓		✓	
Printing & publishing	✓		✓	
Rubber & asbestos		✓		✓
Glass		✓		✓
Metal working machine tools		✓		✓
Textile machinery		✓		✓
Automobiles & parts		✓		✓
Motor cycles & cycles	✓		✓	
Aircraft	✓		✓	
Scientific instruments		✓		✓
Jewellery, silverware	✓		✓	
Games, toys	✓		✓	
B. Industries in which German firms > UK firms				
Footwear		✓		✓
Timber		✓		✓
Leather		✓		✓
Leather products		✓		✓
Plastic		✓		✓
General chemicals		✓		✓
Clay products & pottery		✓		✓
Office machinery		✓		✓
Mining machinery, etc.		✓		✓
Electronic apparatus		✓		✓
Domestic elect. appliances		✓		✓
Watches & clocks		✓		✓

Germany almost invariably has the larger plants, although not always the larger firms. Out of 13 such industries it has larger plants in 11 cases and larger firms in 7.

2 Plant concentration ratios

As with the 4-firm concentration ratios similarities are also evident in the rank-order of industries in terms of the 20-plant concentration ratios. Indeed, if anything the similarity is rather more marked. The regression equations are shown in Table 4.4.

Table 4.4 *Regression equations of 20-plant concentration ratios in pairs of countries, 1963*

Regression equation	Constant	Regression coefficient	Correlation coefficient	Number of industries
UK on Germany	19.4 (4.9)	+ 0.607 (0.111)	0.63	47
UK on France	12.9 (4.8)	+ 0.822 (0.118)	0.72	47
UK on Italy	22.5 (4.8)	+ 0.520 (0.105)	0.59	47
Germany on France	8.2 (3.4)	+ 0.859 (0.082)	0.75	87
Germany on Italy	9.9 (2.9)	+ 0.770 (0.063)	0.80	87
France on Italy	11.0 (2.6)	+ 0.657 (0.057)	0.77	97

Note: The regression equation in each case is $C_i^j = a + bC_i^k$, where C_i^j and C_i^k are the 20-plant employment concentration ratios in the ith industry in country j and country k, respectively.

More significant, however, is the greater similarity between the UK and other countries in the average level of plant concentration as compared to firm concentration. This is evident in the employment weighted plant concentration ratios shown in Table 4.5, and also in Figures 4.1 to 4.3.

Table 4.5 *Employment weighted average 20-plant concentration ratios, 1963*

Country	Number of industries	Concentration
UK	41	30.2
Germany	41	29.0
France	41	27.9
Italy	41	24.3
UK	47	34.7
Germany	47	32.8
France	47	32.2
Italy	47	27.6
Germany	87	32.0
France	87	31.0
Italy	87	26.0

To pursue this point further, we have, for the UK, Germany and France, compared directly the size of the largest four enterprises with that of the largest four plants, and have divided the latter into the former by industry, in order to obtain the number of plants the largest four enterprises would possess if each plant were of the average size of the four largest in the industry.[1] The purpose here is to see how far the size of firm can be explained by the size of plant. In other words, the latter

[1] It is a frequent practice among writers in this field to take the average size of a small number of the largest plants as a proxy for the optimal size of plant. We ourselves have misgivings about whether this is a meaningful device, but those who wish to interpret the analysis in those terms are of course perfectly at liberty to do so.

Fig. 4.1 *20-Plant concentration ratios, 47 industries, UK/Germany*

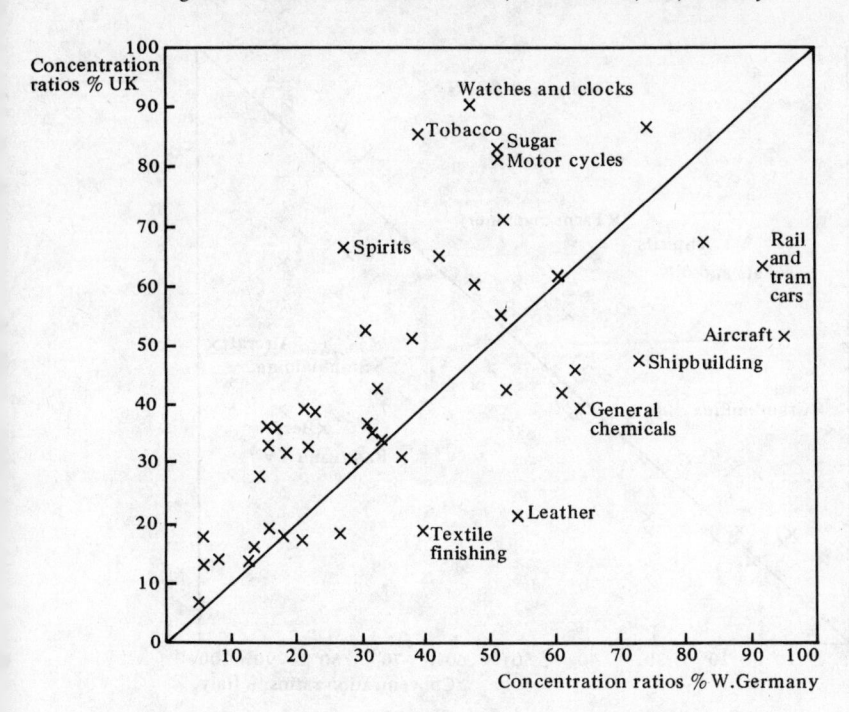

Fig. 4.2 *20-Plant concentration ratios, 47 industries, UK/France*

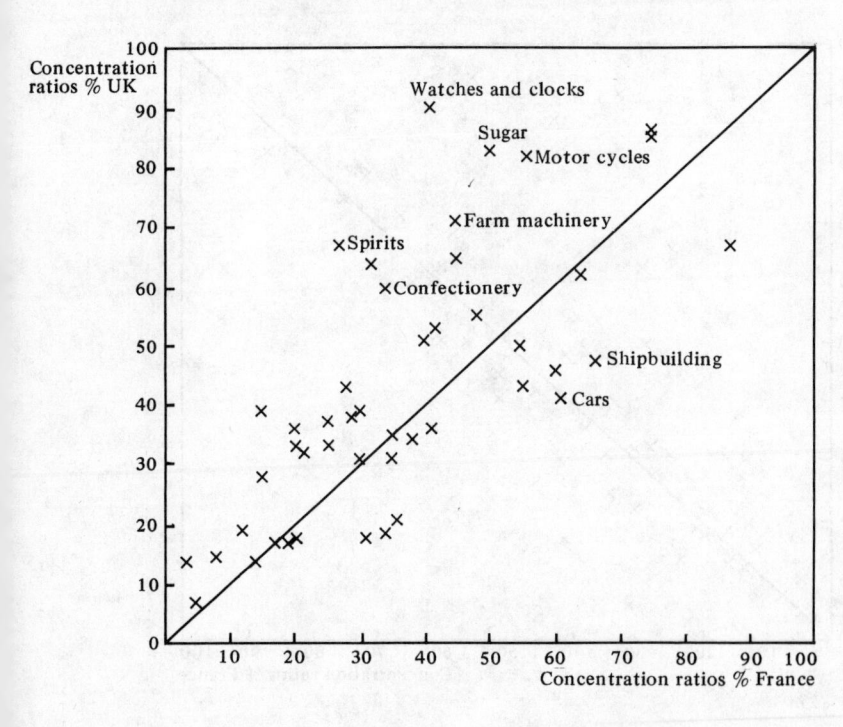

Fig. 4.3 *20-Plant concentration ratios, 47 industries, UK/Italy*

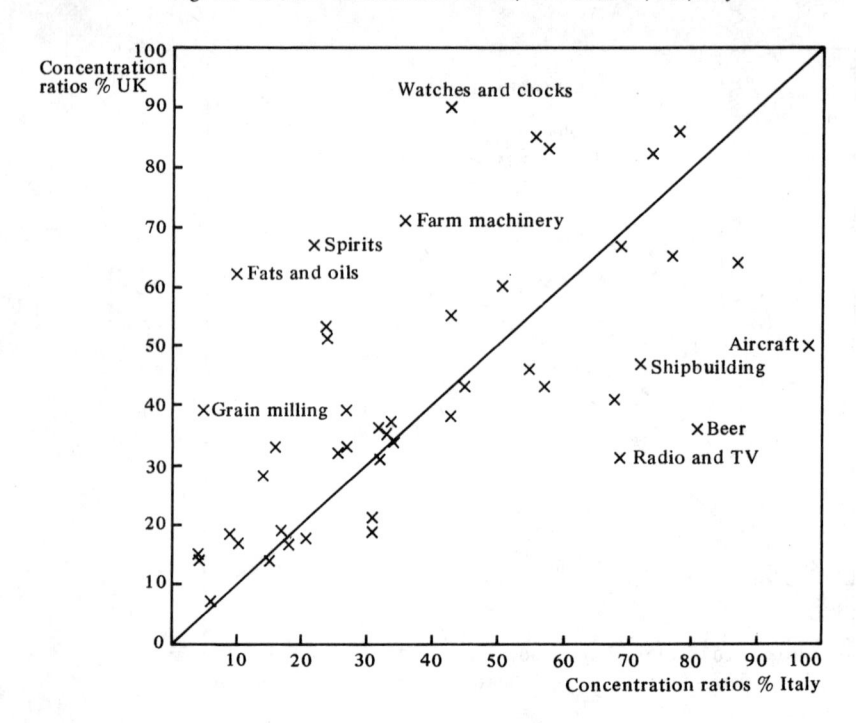

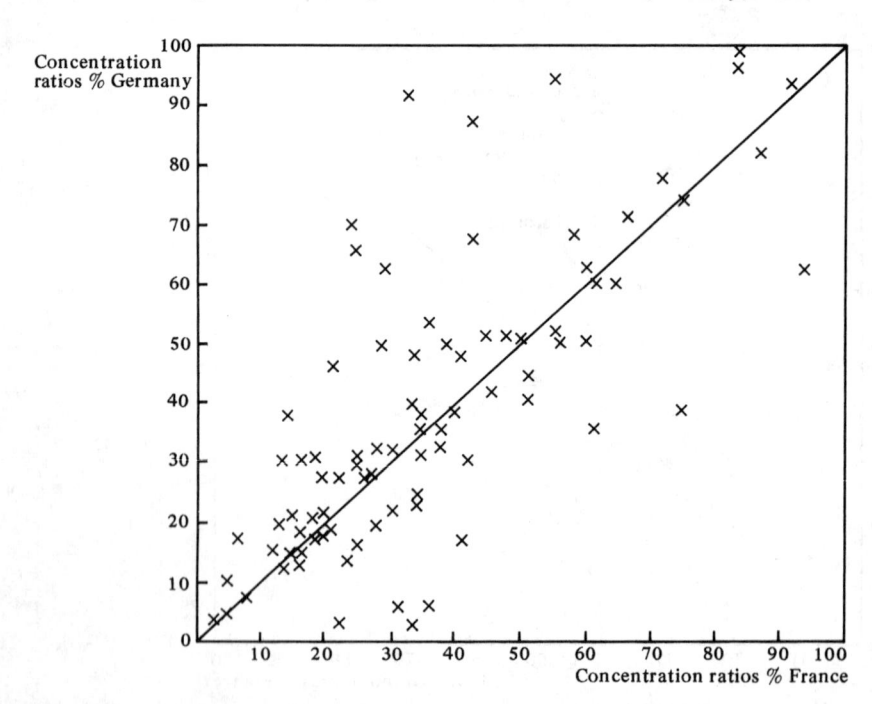

Fig. 4.4 *20-Plant concentration ratios, 87 industries, Germany/France*

Fig. 4.5 *20-Plant concentration ratios, 87 industries, Germany/Italy*

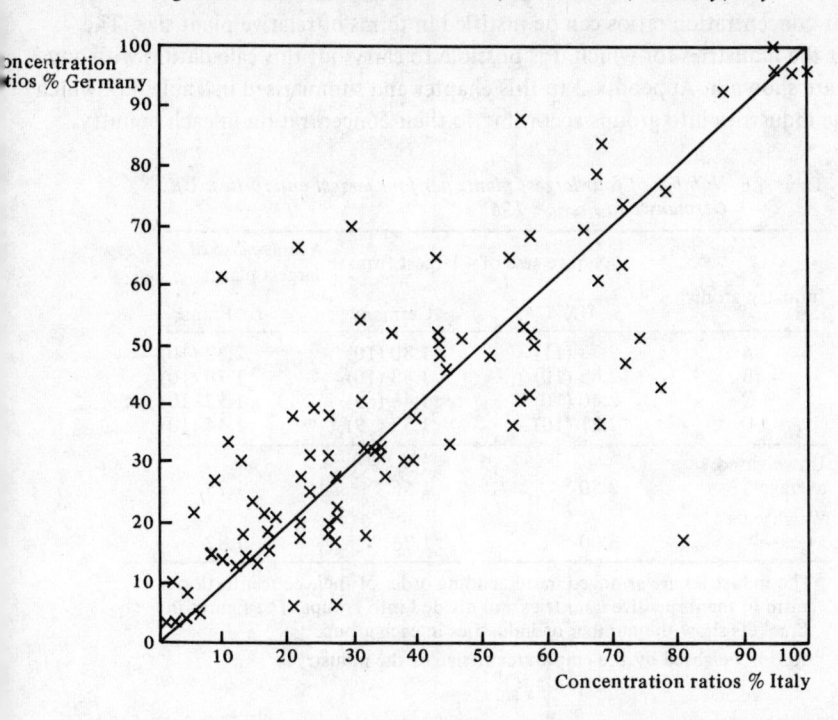

Fig. 4.6 *20-Plant concentration ratios, 97 industries, industries, France/Italy*

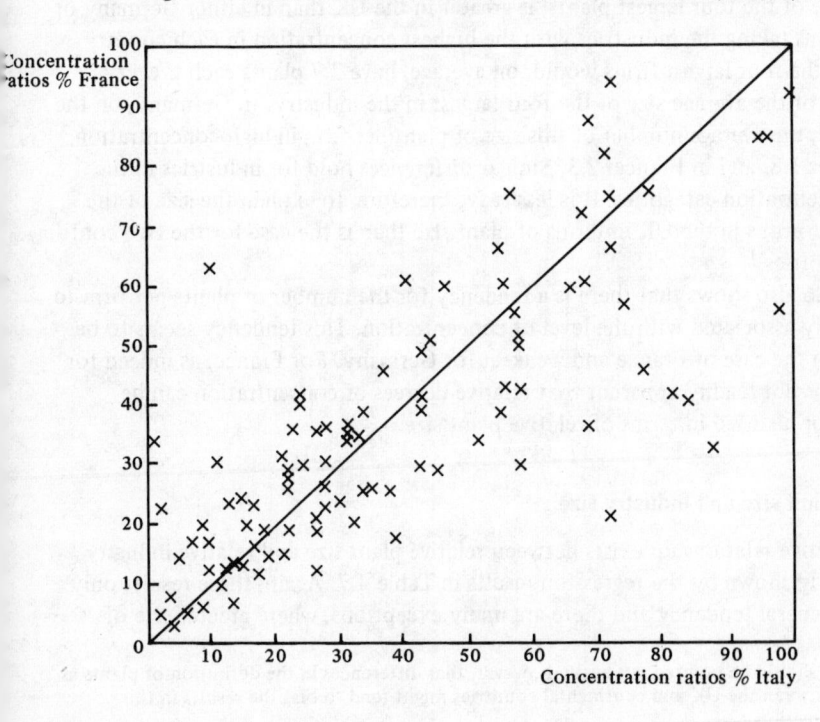

imposes a lower limit on the former. As a related issue we have examined the question of how far concentration ratios can be justified in terms of relative plant size. The results for the industries for which it is possible to carry out this calculation with any accuracy are shown in Appendix 2 to this chapter and summarised in Table 4.6, which divides the industries into groups according to their concentration in each country.

Table 4.6 *Number of four largest plants per four largest enterprises: UK, Germany and France, 1963*

Industry group[a]	Average size of 4 largest firms ÷ Average size of 4 largest plants		
	UK	Germany	France
A	2.73 (11)	1.80 (10)	2.32 (10)
B	2.63 (10)	1.43 (10)	1.70 (10)
C	2.40 (10)	1.46 (9)	1.52 (10)
D	2.21 (10)	1.53 (9)	1.44 (10)
Unweighted average	2.50	1.56	1.75
Weighted average[b]	3.00	1.76	1.87

[a] The industries are arranged in descending order of their concentration ratio in the respective countries and divided into groups. The figures in brackets show the number of industries in each group.

[b] Ratios weighted by the employment size of the industry.

The table shows that, in general, the size of firms, in terms of multiples of the average size of the four largest plants, is greater in the UK than in either Germany or France. Thus taking the industries with the highest concentration in each country, in the UK the four largest firms would, on average, have 2.7 plants each if every plant were of the average size of the four largest in the industry. In Germany, on the other hand, the average number of this size of plant per firm in high concentration industries is 1.8, and in France, 2.3. Similar differences hold for industries in the lower concentration categories. It is less easy, therefore, to explain the size of the largest enterprises in the UK in terms of plant size than is the case for the two continental countries.[1]

Table 4.6 also shows that there is a tendency for the number of plants per firm to be positively associated with the level of concentration. This tendency seems to be strongest in the case of France and weakest for Germany. For France, as indeed for the UK, it is not readily apparent that relative degrees of concentration can be explained or justified in terms of relative plant size.

3 Plant size and industry size

That a positive relationship exists between relative plant size and relative industry size is clearly shown by the regression results in Table 4.7. Again, these results only express a general tendency and there are many exceptions, where greater size of

1 It should be pointed out again, however, that differences in the definition of plants as between the UK and continental countries might tend to bias the results in this direction.

plant is not coupled with larger size of industry. Thus looking at the UK : Germany comparison in more detail Table 4.8 shows that out of 47 cases larger plants are associated with larger industries in 35 industries, so that there are 12 cases (about a quarter of the total) which are exceptions to the general rule. Most of these occur in the food, drink and tobacco and wearing apparel trades, where the UK has larger plants but, very often, smaller industries.

Table 4.7 *Regression equations of plant size on industry size, pairs of countries, 1963*

Regression equation[a]	Constant		Regression coefficient	Correlation coefficient	n
UK on Germany	0.69	+	0.504 (0.059)	0.78	47
UK on France	0.98	+	0.711 (0.137)	0.59	50
Germany on France	0.94	+	0.571 (0.051)	0.78	84
Germany on Italy	1.52	+	0.409 (0.047)	0.70	82
France on Italy	0.94	+	0.262 (0.033)	0.66	85

[a] The dependent variable is the ratio of plant size and the independent variable the ratio of industry size as between pairs of countries.

Table 4.8 *Relative size of plant and industry, 47 industries in UK and West Germany, 1963*

Industry size	UK plants bigger[a]	German plants bigger[a]	Total
UK industry size bigger	12	2	14
Germany industry size bigger	9	23	32 (+1)[b]
Total	21	25	46 (+1)[b]

[a] Based on a comparison of the average size of the 20 largest plants in each country.

[b] In one case the German industry size exceeds that of the UK but plants are of equal size.

4 Plant concentration ratios and industry size

Finally we have examined the relationship between plant concentration ratios and industry size. The results are shown in Table 4.9. There is certainly a negative association between the two variables although it is not particularly strong. Nevertheless it is a closer association than the one found for the 4-firm concentration ratios.

5 Further analysis of plant size – the UK and West Germany 1958 to 1968

In addition to the above analysis it has also been possible to compare the average size of the largest plants (i.e. those employing 1000 or more) in the UK and West Germany at the two-digit level over the period 1958 to 1968. The reconciliation of the UK with the German industrial classification is shown in Appendix 4.3.

For the UK it has been observed (Armstrong and Silberston, 1965) that for most manufacturing sectors there was a steady increase in the importance of large plants

Table 4.9 *Regression equations of plant concentration ratios on industry size, pairs of countries, 1963*

Regression equation[a]	Constant	Regression coefficient	Correlation coefficient	n
UK on Germany	1.45	−0.126 (0.058)	0.30	47
UK on France	1.62	−0.175 (0.062)	0.38	50
Germany on France	1.46	−0.113 (0.024)	0.47	83
Germany on Italy	1.61	−0.110 (0.033)	0.35	81
France on Italy	1.35	−0.116 (0.039)	0.32	81

[a] The dependent variable is the ratio of the 20-plant concentration ratios, and the independent variable – the ratio of industry size.

Table 4.10 *Plants employing 1000 or more, UK and West Germany 1958 and 1968*

Industry sector	UK Number of plants 1958	UK Number of plants 1968	UK Persons engaged as % of total in industry 1958	UK Persons engaged as % of total in industry 1968	W. Germany Number of plants 1958	W. Germany Number of plants 1968	W. Germany Persons engaged as % of total in industry 1958	W. Germany Persons engaged as % of total in industry 1968
Food, drink, tobacco	110	134	29.9	31.7	32	46	11.0	13.8
Textiles	44	56	9.6	14.5	73	57	19.0	17.3
Clothing	13	13	5.0	5.8	13	7	5.7	2.3
Footwear	5	8	7.0	11.5	13	9	27.2	16.6
Wood & furniture	–	3	–	1.4	–	8	–	4.2
Paper	16	19	31.5	36.3	12	12	22.4	24.7
Paper products	11	17	13.5	14.9	4	8	6.5	10.2
Printing & publishing	38	33	21.4	19.6	4	13	3.2	9.3
Rubber & asbestos	26	30	46.0	52.2	24	26	60.9	59.2
Chemicals & allied	82	90	40.8	42.2	82	103	59.7	61.2
Pottery, etc.	16	16	9.9	11.5	25	18	9.5	8.8
Glass	14	19	44.2	48.5	10	17	28.2	39.4
Metals	111	105	51.7	53.2	118	119	66.3	68.6
Metal products	35	56	11.9	14.9	47	43	15.6	12.9
Mechanical engineering	168	163	35.8	31.2	192	213	43.1	38.2
Instrument engineering	19	31	26.3	31.0	22	26	36.8	36.3
Electrical engineering	149	187	59.6	56.1	146	214	55.2	54.6
Vehicles & aircraft	184	170	75.1	73.9	60	86	78.5	82.8
Shipbuilding	64	35	67.2	63.3	17	15	72.5	76.8
All manufacturing	1128	1198	34.1	34.5	916	1065	34.5	36.5

from the inter-war years to 1958. This section looks at the trend in the relative importance of large plants – i.e. those employing 1000 or more – in the UK and West Germany, over the period 1958 to 1968. The relevant calculations are shown in Tables 4.10 and 4.11, and in Appendix 4.4. The main results may be summarized as follows.

First, for manufacturing industry as a whole the UK has a slightly larger number of large plants than Germany – thus in 1968 the UK had 1198 such plants as compared to Germany's 1065. The higher UK number is accounted for in the main,

Table 4.11 *Ratios of average plant size, plant employing 1000 or more, UK and West Germany, 1958, 1963 and 1968*

Industry sector	1958	Year 1963	1968
Food, drink, tobacco	1.11	1.10	1.16
Textiles	1.13	1.14	1.09
Clothing	1.15	1.26	1.25
Footwear	0.68	0.90	0.82
Wood & furniture	–	1.26	0.76
Paper	1.05	1.06	0.97
Paper products	1.00	1.09	0.84
Printing & publishing	1.25	1.15	1.26
Rubber & asbestos	0.92	0.95	0.87
Chemicals	0.66	0.60	0.60
Pottery, etc.	1.04	0.90	0.97
Glass	0.92	0.87	0.88
Metals	0.80	0.74	0.78
Metal products	0.95	0.95	0.86
Mechanical engineering	0.88	0.84	0.82
Instrument engineering	0.67	0.74	0.78
Electrical engineering	1.07	1.07	0.93
Vehicles & aircraft	0.73	0.65	0.64
Shipbuilding	0.62	0.76	0.85
All manufacturing	0.91	0.86	0.84

however, by the relatively large number of UK plants in two sectors – Food, drink, tobacco, and vehicles and aircraft. Altogether there are 11 out of 19 sectors in which the UK has the larger number of large plants in 1968. The German advantage in terms of numbers is mainly in mechanical and electrical engineering and, but to a lesser extent, in chemicals and metals.

Second, the proportion of the workforce engaged in large plants has not shown a great deal of change in either country. Over the ten year period 1958 to 68 there was a very small increase in the UK from 34.1 per cent to 34.5 per cent, but the 1968 figure was lower than that for 1963 when the figure was 35.1 per cent. The decline over the latter period is particularly interesting in view of the marked rise in enterprise concentration which occurred in a great many industries. This rise was associated with a marked acceleration in merger activity one of the principal justifications of which, as claimed by many commentators as well as interested parties, was to promote the realisation of economies of scale. Certainly such economies have not generally been achieved through increases in the employment size of plants. Even more surprising perhaps is the finding that the decline in the proportion of the labour-force engaged in large plants seems, judging by the results of the 1971 Census of Production, to have continued in the period after 1968.[1] In Germany the incease has been more noticeable and more persistent – from 34.5 per cent in 1958 to 35.9 per cent in 1963, to 36.5 per cent in 1968, and to 37.1 per cent in 1971 – but again it has been modest. Similarly the individual sectors have not, in general, experienced a marked change in the percentage of persons engaged in the larger plants over this period in either country.

Thirdly, the average size of large plants decreased over the ten year period in the UK from 2,350 to 2,260 but increased in Germany, from 2,580 to 2,700. The

1 The 1971 Census, however, is not entirely comparable with earlier years.

comparison is shown most clearly in Table 4.11 which shows the ratios of average plant size for the two countries. For all manufacturing the average size of large plants in the UK in 1958 was 91 per cent of the average size in Germany. In 1968 UK plants were on average only 84 per cent of the size of their German counterparts. Over the period as a whole the UK plant size relative to the German decreased in 13 out of the 19 manufacturing sectors and showed a significant increase in only three cases – footwear, instrument engineering and shipbuilding. The superiority of the German position in terms of plant size was, in 1968, particularly marked in wood and furniture, chemicals, metals, instrument engineering and vehicles. These results confirm those of of G.F. Ray (1966) who found that the average employment size of plants with a thousand or more persons engaged in the two countries in 1958 was larger on average in Germany than in Britain.

This comparison is, however, in terms of the average size of all plants employing 1000 or more in both countries. As we have seen the number of such plants differs widely as between the two countries in a number of sectors which implies that the above analysis may be misleading. To be specific, one country might, for a given industry, have a greater proportion of the workforce engaged in plants employing 1000 or more than the other but those plants might also be smaller in average size; alternatively, a relatively large average size of large plants might be coupled with a relatively low concentration of employment in such plants. It is more appropriate, therefore, to compare average sizes for a given number of plants in the two countries. The results of this comparison are shown in Table 4.12. The figures on the left hand side of the table show the number of plants for which the comparison is made for each industry in each year. They are, in fact, the number of plants employing 1000 or more in Germany. It should be noted that tests indicated that changes over time in the number of plants being compared made hardly any difference to the results, in the sense that the relative pattern remained the same.

As compared in Table 4.11 the relative size of plants in the UK is, of course, increased in industries where, on the basis of the Table 4.11 comparison, the number of plants is greater in the UK, and reduced in industries where the number of plants is greater in Germany. Because the UK has a larger number of large plants in the majority of industries, the net result is to increase the relative size of UK plants. Thus, whereas in 1958 the previous comparison showed that the average size of plant for all manufacturing was smaller in the UK than in Germany, the comparison based on the same number of plants shows the UK to have, on average, marginally larger plants in that year. Again, in 1968 Table 4.12 shows that there were 7 sectors in which UK plants were on average bigger than their German counterparts, whereas in Table 4.11 this was so of only 4 sectors.

However, as far as *changes* in relative size are concerned the picture is very much the same as before. From having, on average, slightly larger plants than West Germany in 1958 the average size of UK manufacturing plants fell to 89 per cent of the average German size by 1968. The relative size of UK plants decreased in 12 out of the 19 sectors and improved significantly in only 4 – textiles, clothing, footwear, and instrument engineering. The German supremacy in 1968 is again seen to be particularly marked in wood and furniture, chemicals and metals, and also in mechanical engineering.

The larger size of German plants would, in view of the higher labour productivity,

Table 4.12 *Ratios of average plant sizes, UK : West Germany, 1958, 1963, 1968* [a]

Industry sector	Number of plants[b] 1958	1963	1968	Size ratio UK : WG 1958	1963	1968
Food, drink, tobacco	32	38	46	1.95	1.85	1.87
Textiles	73	65	57	0.73	0.71	0.85
Clothing	13	8	7	1.15	1.50	1.54
Footwear	13	11	9	0.49	0.66	0.79
Wood and furniture	–	9	8	–	0.84	0.62
Paper	12	12	12	1.16	1.20	1.12
Paper products	4	6	8	1.33	1.51	1.31
Printing and publishing	4	8	13	2.95	2.24	1.87
Rubber and asbestos	24	26	26	0.96	0.99	0.95
Chemicals	82	96	103	0.66	0.57	0.56
Pottery, etc.	25	19	18	0.91	0.86	0.92
Glass	10	17	17	1.10	0.93	0.92
Metals	118	127	119	0.77	0.69	0.72
Metal products	47	50	43	0.85	0.96	0.92
Mechanical engineering	192	217	213	0.82	0.74	0.71
Instrument engineering	22	24	26	0.64	0.76	0.83
Electrical engineering	146	208	214	1.09	0.93	0.86
Vehicles and aircraft	60	80	86	1.38	1.11	1.00
Shipbuilding	17	13	15	1.42	1.45	1.50
All manufacturing	916	1048	1065	1.02	0.93	0.89

[a] The size ratios have been calculated for the number of plants shown in the left hand columns of the table.

[b] These are the number of German plants in each trade employing 1000 or more.

Table 4.13 *Comparison of net output per head in plants employing 1000 or more 1967/68* [a]
(Ratios of German net output/head to UK net output/head)

Industry sector	Exchange rate 9.56DM = £1.[b]	Excahnge rate 11.22DM = £1.[c]
Food and drink	131.8	113.2
Textiles	104.0	89.3
Clothing	189.2	162.4
Footwear	116.7	100.2
Wood and furniture	152.4	130.9
Paper	125.9	108.1
Paper products	113.7	97.7
Printing and publishing	116.6	100.2
Rubber and asbestos	119.7	102.8
Chemicals and allied	140.0	120.3
Pottery, etc.	144.7	124.3
Glass	146.1	125.5
Metals	136.0	116.8
Metal products	130.5	112.1
Mechanical engineering	115.1	98.9
Scientific instruments	117.0	100.5
Electrical engineering	119.8	102.9
Vehicles and aircraft	139.7	120.0
Shipbuilding	138.5	119.0
All manufacturing	131.0	112.6

[a] The UK data refer to 1968 and the West German data to 1967.

[b] Average official exchange rate, 1968.

[c] Average official exchange rate, 1967.

be considerably more marked if the comparison were made instead on the basis of an output measure of size. Table 4.13 gives an indication of the extent to which the value of net output per head in Germany exceeds that in the UK. The difficulty in using such a measure is that the results vary greatly depending on the rate of exchange used. The official rate of exchange is unlikely to reflect accurately the pattern of relative prices and the tentative nature of the results must be borne in mind when drawing any conclusions.

Since the UK data refer to 1968 and the German data to 1967, Table 4.13 gives two sets of figures: one based on the average official rate of exchange between the DM and the £ in 1968, and the other on the average exchange rate in 1967. The big change in the exchange rate as a result of the devaluation of the pound in November 1967 results in a big difference in the estimated ratios of net output per head. But whereas it would be unwise to attach too much importance to any one set of figures it is interesting to observe the sectors in which higher German productivity is particularly marked. These are, clothing, wood and furniture, chemicals, pottery, glass, metals, vehicles, and shipbuilding.

The decline in the relative size of plant in the UK is probably linked with the slow growth of the UK market and it is worth exploring a little further the relationship between plant size, economies of scale and the rate of market expansion. An important benefit of rapidly expanding markets is that they give an inducement to businessmen to invest in capacity extensions of minimum optimal size. Given, that is, the minimum optimal size of plant, the faster the growth of the market the more likely it is that the competitive process will yield satisfactory results in terms of plant scale and plant scale economies. When the minimum optimal size of plant is large in relation to the annual rate of market expansion a firm which invests in such a plant will realise that the additional sales necessary to render the investment profitable will have to come to a large extent by capturing part of the market share of competitors. Whether or not the investment will take place will depend on the competitiveness of the industry, but in many oligopolistic situations firms may well invest in sub-optimal extensions of capacity in order to minimise the danger of excess capacity and the price-cutting consequences. With a high rate of market expansion on the other hand, the additional sales needed to operate an optimal sized plant efficiently will depend less on the transfer of sales and will be achieved more completely by general sales expansion. The importance of all this for efficiency depends of course on the size of plant specific economies of scale in individual markets.

Similarly, a fast rate of expansion may lead to benefits in terms of the degree of specialisation *within* plants. Rapidly expanding markets will tend to encourage specialisation and so yield benefits of longer production runs. Slow growth on the other hand may encourage the diversification of activities within the plant. Where a number of competitors have followed such a strategy and have diversified into one another's markets substantial economies of specialisation may be lost. Furthermore, in this case the competitive process may not be able to achieve a satisfactory solution, because if one firm decides to increase specialisation and attempts to extend the production of selected products by means of price reductions it may result in competitive responses from other firms with the result that no significant increase in specialisation is achieved. Competitive environments of this kind are likely to foster some kind of co-operative agreement between firms, or to encourage mergers and acquisitions, as a means of achieving a more acceptable relationship between the firm and its environment.

6 Size of plant and output per head

Finally, comparisons have been made of the relationship between labour productivity, as measured by net output per head, and size of plant for the UK and West Germany. The results are shown in Table 4.14.

Table 4.14 *Index numbers of net output per head, by size of plant, UK and West Germany*

Industry sector	UK 1968			W. Germany 1967		
	Size of plant			Size of plant		
	200–499	500–999	1000 & above	200–499	500–999	1000 & above
Food and Drink	100	108.5	123.4	100	129.5	83.2
Textiles[b]	100	119.6	177.3	100	98.6	100.8
Clothing	100	101.0	111.2	100	110.8	140.1
Footwear	100	94.5	120.1	100	105.4	99.6
Wood and furniture	100	113.9	94.0	100	100.6	99.5
Paper	100	88.0	110.8	100	122.1	100.2
Paper products	100	98.3	107.1	100	110.2	99.7
Printing and publishing	100	112.3	122.3	100	112.7	129.1
Rubber and asbestos	100	123.0	124.3	100	106.3	120.2
Chemicals and allied[b]	100	109.2	103.5	100	106.4	121.2
Pottery etc.	100	93.3	87.6	100	84.3	83.6
Glass	100	116.3	122.4	100	127.6	138.2
Metals	100	107.1	112.6	100	110.5	121.1
Metal products	100	96.4	104.1	100	106.3	106.0
Mechanical engineering	100	104.0	106.5	100	105.5	102.8
Scientific instruments	100	102.8	97.2	100	95.1	105.2
Electrical engineering	100	109.2	113.9	100	98.6	107.2
Vehicles and aircraft	100	108.7	118.5	100	96.5	119.5
Shipbuilding	100	99.2	88.1	100	110.3	98.0
All manufacturing[a]	100	109.8	117.4	100	106.7	113.0

[a] For Germany, excluding oil refining and tobacco. In both cases net output and net output per head are abnormally large for plants employing 500–999. Their inclusion in the German all manufacturing figures increases the 1967 net output per head for this size class of plants to 126.1 and reduces the index for the largest size class to 107.4. For the UK case oil refining and tobacco are included in the 'all manufacturing' figure. Excluding oil refining results in a very slight increase in the productivity index of the larger plants – to 110.1 and 117.6 respectively. For tobacco details are given only for plants employing 200 or more, but net output per head for these is not out of line with that for other trades, so that it is unlikely that excluding tobacco would make much difference to the overall result.

[b] There is a major difference in the coverage of these sectors. The UK includes man-made fibres in textiles whereas Germany includes it in Chemicals. No information is given on the man-made fibres industry in the UK 1968 Census and so no entirely satisfactory comparison is possible. This probably has little effect on the comparative figures for Chemicals but is certainly important in textiles, as is apparent if the 1963 figures for man-made fibres are excluded from UK 'textiles'. The index numbers then become 119.2 and 143.1 respectively.

The general conclusion emerging from the table is that there is no tendency, as found by Ray for 1954, for the largest German plants to show superior labour productivity levels over smaller plants relative to the British pattern. In fact, for manufacturing as a whole, the tendency is the reverse of this, the productivity differential between the UK plants being greater than that for Germany. For individual trades there is a fairly even division, the difference between large and small plants being greater in Germany in 10, and in the UK in 9, of the 19 industrial sectors.

For many of the individual industries the relationship between productivity and plant size is similar for the two countries. But there are one or two distinctly 'odd' results – the very high productivity in the largest UK textile plants, for instance, which in part is due to the inclusion of man-made fibres which, in Germany, is included in the chemicals sector.[1]

7   Summary of main conclusions

The main conclusions of this chapter may be summarised as follows:

(i) The relative size of German plants *vis à vis* British plants is much greater than the size of German firms relative to British firms. German plants are in fact generally larger and often substantially so in such fields as engineering, metals, and vehicles. The UK advantage in terms of plant size is found in food, drink, tobacco, wearing apparel and paper products.

(ii) The ranking of industries by average size of the 20 largest plants is similar for all countries. So also is the ranking by plant concentration ratio, which suggests the importance of technical factors in determining plant size.

(iii) More striking, however, is that the UK and other EEC countries are more similar with respect to plant concentration levels than with respect to the level of firm concentration.

(iv) There is a strong positive association between relative plant size and relative industry size.

(v) Leading UK firms are in general larger in relation to the average size of the 4-leading plants in each industry than is the case for Germany or France. It is therefore more difficult to explain the size of the largest firms in the UK in terms of plant size than it is in the case of Germany and France.

(vi) At the 2-digit level a comparison of large plants in the UK and West Germany over the period 1958 to 68 shows that although the UK has a slightly larger number of such plants in maufacturing as a whole its superiority in this respect is mainly in the fields of food, drink and tobacco and vehicles and aircraft, while Germany leads in mechanical and electrical engineering, chemicals and metals.

(vii) As far as the relative size of large plants is concerned UK plants declined in size relative to German ones over the ten year period. This is true whether the comparison is of the average size of all plants employing 1000 or more or of the same number of plants in the two countries. The superiority of the German position in terms of plant size is particularly marked in chemicals, metals, engineering and vehicles – a finding which also applied to the analysis on the basis of a finer industry breakdown.

(viii) Finally, there was no observable tendency for the largest German plants to show superior labour productivity levels over smaller plants as compared to UK pattern. Indeed for manufacturing as a whole if anything the reverse seems to be the case.

1   See footnote to Table 4.14 above.

Appendix 4.1 *Average size of the 20 largest plants by industry, UK, Germany, France and Italy, 1963*

Industry	Average plant size ('000)				Ratios of average plant size			
	UK	Germany	France	Italy	UK: WG	UK: France	Germany: France	Germany: Italy
Automobiles	8.97	13.55	9.11	4.41	0.66	0.98	1.49	3.07
Aircraft	6.33	1.23	2.65	0.59	5.15	2.39	0.46	2.08
Iron and steel	6.18	9.90	5.90	2.95	0.62	1.05	1.68	3.36
Motor generators	5.49	5.52	1.92	0.92	0.99	2.87	2.89	6.00
Shipbuilding	4.75	3.24	3.28	1.85	1.47	1.45	0.99	1.75
Electronics	3.78	5.92	1.54	0.80	0.64	2.45	3.84	7.40
Rubber and asbestos	3.05	3.22	2.50	1.52	0.95	1.22	1.29	2.12
Confectionery	2.76	1.30	0.46	0.56	2.12	6.00	2.83	2.32
Basic metals	2.62	9.44	1.83	1.92	0.28	1.43	5.16	4.92
Printing and publishing	2.58	1.78	1.23	0.83	1.45	2.10	1.45	2.14
Railroad cars	2.47	1.03	1.00	0.95	2.40	2.47	1.03	1.08
Non ferrous metals	2.29	2.12	1.02	0.87	1.08	2.25	2.08	2.44
Domestic elect. appliances	2.15	2.55	0.73	1.32	0.84	2.95	3.49	1.93
Bread	1.91	0.80	0.46	0.63	2.39	4.15	1.74	1.27
Steel tubes	1.87	2.32	0.93	1.41	0.81	2.01	2.49	1.65
Glass	1.85	1.91	1.19	0.61	0.97	1.55	1.61	3.13
Tobacco	1.84	0.97	0.51	0.74	1.90	3.61	1.90	1.31
Farm machinery	1.71	2.20	0.90	0.38	0.78	1.90	2.44	5.79
Beer and malt	1.57	0.85	0.42	0.25	1.85	3.74	2.02	3.40
Mining machinery	1.57	3.23	0.69	0.50	0.49	2.28	4.68	6.46
Pulp and paper	1.55	1.27	0.91	0.76	1.22	1.70	1.40	1.67
Clothing	1.40	1.11	0.75	0.93	1.26	1.87	1.48	1.19
Paper and board products	1.31	0.94	0.44	0.34	1.39	2.98	2.14	2.76
Canned fruit and veg.	1.30	0.32	0.35	0.62	4.06	3.71	0.91	0.52
Office machines	1.30	2.32	1.08	0.98	0.56	1.20	2.15	2.37
Metal cutting machine tools	1.15	1.65	0.68	0.62	0.70	1.69	2.43	2.66
Baked clay products	1.14	1.55	0.68	0.32	0.74	1.68	1.63	1.22
Textile machinery	1.12	1.88	0.43	0.78	0.60	2.60	4.37	2.41
Hosiery	1.06	1.00	0.79	0.62	1.06	1.34	1.27	1.61
Motor cycles, cycles	1.01	0.70	0.33	0.98	1.44	3.06	2.12	0.71
Footwear	0.93	1.40	0.86	0.47	0.66	1.08	1.63	2.98
Furniture	0.74	0.99	0.36	0.27	0.75	2.06	2.75	3.67
Games, toys	0.73	0.47	0.35	0.16	1.55	2.09	1.34	2.94
Sugar	0.66	0.38	0.57	0.51	1.74	1.16	0.67	0.75
Plastic	0.63	1.11	0.44	0.40	0.57	1.43	2.52	2.78
Corn milling	0.62	0.28	0.17	0.11	2.21	3.65	1.65	2.55
Textile finishing	0.61	0.88	0.69	0.61	0.69	0.88	1.28	1.44
Soft drinks	0.60	0.27	0.10	0.22	2.22	6.00	2.70	1.23
Alcohol, etc.	0.57	0.31	0.35	0.20	1.84	1.63	0.89	1.55
Timber	0.55	0.79	0.53	–	0.70	1.04	1.49	–
Animal and veg. fats and oils	0.47	0.51	0.44	0.20	0.92	1.07	1.16	2.55
Watches and clocks	0.45	0.87	0.41	0.22	0.52	1.10	2.12	3.95
Jewellery, etc.	0.43	0.35	0.22	0.24	1.23	1.95	1.59	1.46
Leather	0.27	0.85	0.36	0.33	0.32	0.75	2.36	2.58
Leather products	0.27	0.41	0.28	0.20	0.66	0.96	1.46	2.05
Mattresses and bedding	0.25	0.25	0.17	0.11	1.00	1.47	1.47	2.27
Fur	0.16	0.14	0.09	0.12	1.14	1.78	1.56	1.17

Appendix 4.2 *4-firm and 4-plant concentration ratios, UK, Germany and France, 1963*

	4-firm concentration ratio			4-plant concentration ratio			4-firm / 4-plant		
	UK	WG	France	UK	WG	France	UK	WG	France
Sugar	95	41	42	42	15	22	2.22	2.82	2.10
Tobacco	88	34	100	33	13	18	2.45	2.86	–
Watches and clocks	66	29	24	46	23	20	1.37	1.31	1.19
Aircraft	65	59	57	18	42	20	3.65	1.48	2.65
Motor cycles	65	25	43	45	21	27	1.47	1.20	1.48
Alcohol	58	13	13	31	11	9	1.75	1.21	1.51
Office machinery	54	53	67	31	35	43	1.71	1.57	1.69
Grain milling	51	10	10	16	9	7	3.10	1.20	1.44
Bread, biscuits	48	4	15	6	3	10	8.20	1.21	1.42
Glass	48	21	39	18	14	15	2.63	1.34	2.64
Confectionery	47	25	15	32	19	12	1.47	1.33	1.20
Textile machinery	45	28	23	25	24	23	1.76	1.20	1.05
General chemicals	44	38	35	13	33	11	3.43	1.30	3.05
Beer and malt	41	7	24	9	5	15	4.46	1.31	1.67
Domestic elect. app.	40	28	25	27	21	16	1.51	1.18	1.42
Autos and parts	40	39	50	16	28	38	2.56	1.36	1.42
Soft drinks	40	15	22	14	–	9	3.00	–	2.99
Games, toys	38	18	11	17	16	9	2.13	1.14	1.24
Canned frozen food	35	12	15	15	8	9	2.37	1.37	1.91
Paper and Board	35	25	26	11	11	12	3.11	2.40	2.25
Rubber and asbestos	35	34	50	18	31	32	1.95	1.14	1.55
Electronic apparatus	33	37	43	11	13	11	3.11	3.05	4.34
Jewellery, etc.	27	11	9	12	8	8	2.23	1.33	1.14
Textile finishing	24	15	37	6	13	15	4.29	1.11	2.32
Metal working tools	22	8	13	11	8	7	2.09	1.00	1.85
Scientific instrs.	21	17	22	11	15	18	1.89	1.08	1.23
Mattresses and bedding	21	18	25	10	13	14	1.88	1.39	1.79
Fur	21	8	15	16	8	8	1.15	1.01	1.28
Paper and board products	17	12	5	7	5	4	2.19	2.17	1.20
Wool	16	14	14	5	–	13	2.86	–	1.09
Footwear	16	19	13	6	11	7	2.35	1.75	1.95
Hosiery	16	10	7	5	4	5	3.02	2.32	1.41
Printg. and publishg.	16	6	7	5	5	5	3.18	1.26	1.43
Mining machinery	15	21	14	12	14	8	1.26	1.36	1.72
Wood furniture	15	4	3	6	3	2	2.55	1.21	1.34
Clay and pottery	13	18	14	6	–	7	2.18	–	1.98
Leather and tanning	12	39	16	6	34	11	1.86	1.19	1.47
Leather products	12	5	6	9	5	5	1.40	1.06	1.18
Plastic	11	10	6	6	7	6	1.99	1.35	1.00
Clothing	9	4	2	3	1	1	3.33	3.21	1.93
Timber	6	4	3	4	2	1	1.35	2.52	2.32

Appendix 4.3 *The 1958, 1963 and 1968 comparisons of plant size approximately by industry order : UK and W. Germany*

Source: The UK figures are derived from Census of Production data for 1958, 1963 and 1968.

The German figures are derived from the annual details published in *Statistisches Jahrbuch* (1960, 1965 and 1970 Yearbooks contain the relevant information) and refer to September of each of these three years. The reconciliation of the German industrial classification to a UK industry order basis is as follows:

German industry	UK industry
Food and drink / Tobacco	Food, drink and tobacco
Textiles	Textiles
Clothing	Clothing
Footwear	Footwear
Paper, pulp and fibre	Paper and board
Paper and pulp products	Cardboard boxes etc. plus miscellaneous paper products
Printing and publishing	Printing and publishing
Wood products / Sawmills and wood-working	Timber, furniture, etc.
Glass	Glass
Pottery / Construction materials (including sand and gravel)	Bricks, pottery, cement, etc.
Rubber and asbestos	Rubber plus asbestos
Chemicals / Mineral oil refining / Coal products	Chemicals and allied
Iron production / Iron and steel casting / Wire drawing and cold rolling / Non-ferrous metal production	Metal manufacture
Secondary transformation of steel / Iron, tinplate, metal goods	Metal products not elswhere specified
Steel and light metal construction / Mechanical engineering	Engineering, excluding Electrical goods
Electrical engineering	Electrical goods
Vehicles and aircraft	Vehicles
Shipbuilding	Shipbuilding and marine engineering

Appendix 4.4 *Plants employing 1000 or more, UK, 1958, 1963 and 1968*

Industry sector	Number of plants			Persons engaged as % of total in industry			Average size of plant, '000		
	1958	1963	1968	1958	1963	1968	1958	1963	1968
Food, drink, tobacco	110	124	134	29.9	31.3	31.7	1.97	1.91	1.88
Textiles	44	50	56	9.6	12.2	14.5	1.82	1.79	1.67
Clothing	13	12	13	5.0	5.3	5.8	1.62	1.73	1.55
Footwear	5	5	8	7.0	7.5	11.5	1.50	1.54	1.37
Wood and furniture	–	3	3	–	2.0	1.4	–	1.77	1.20
Paper	16	17	19	31.5	32.0	36.3	1.62	1.66	1.45
Paper products	11	11	17	13.5	13.2	14.9	1.57	1.65	1.39
Printing and publishing	38	37	33	21.4	20.1	19.6	1.86	1.95	2.09
Rubber and asbestos	26	28	30	46.0	49.4	52.2	2.24	2.50	2.52
Chemicals	82	87	90	40.8	41.4	42.2	2.21	2.11	2.11
Pottery, etc.	16	17	16	9.9	11.2	11.5	1.44	1.56	1.59
Glass	14	20	19	44.2	51.3	48.5	2.22	1.85	1.86
Metals	111	115	105	51.7	53.8	53.2	2.65	2.68	2.77
Metal products	35	53	56	11.9	16.7	14.9	1.60	1.60	1.43
Mechanical engineering	168	169	163	35.8	33.1	31.2	2.06	1.99	1.87
Instrument engineering	19	26	31	26.3	33.5	31.0	1.59	1.71	1.71
Electrical engineering	149	168	187	59.6	60.1	56.1	2.61	2.75	2.26
Vehicles and aircraft	184	186	170	75.1	77.0	73.9	3.19	3.28	3.43
Shipbuilding	64	43	35	67.2	68.4	63.3	2.89	3.22	3.39
All manufacturing	1128	1189	1198	34.1	35.1	34.5	2.35	2.35	2.26

Appendix 4.4 (cont'd) *Plants employing 1000 or more, West Germany, 1958, 1963 and 1968*

Industry sector	Number of plants			Persons engaged as % of total in industry			Average size of plant, '000		
	1958	1963	1968	1958	1963	1968	1958	1963	1968
Food, drink, tobacco	32	38	46	11.0	11.6	13.8	1.78	1.73	1.62
Textiles	73	65	57	19.0	17.7	17.3	1.61	1.57	1.53
Clothing	13	8	7	5.7	2.7	2.3	1.41	1.37	1.25
Footwear	13	11	9	27.2	18.6	16.6	2.22	1.72	1.67
Wood and furniture	–	9	8	–	4.0	4.2	–	1.40	1.57
Paper	12	12	12	22.4	23.0	24.7	1.54	1.57	1.49
Paper products	4	6	8	6.5	7.2	10.2	1.61	1.52	1.65
Printing and publishing	4	8	13	3.2	6.1	9.3	1.49	1.69	1.65
Rubber and asbestos	24	26	26	60.9	59.1	59.2	2.43	2.64	2.89
Chemicals and allied	82	96	103	59.7	60.9	61.2	3.36	3.50	3.51
Pottery, etc.	25	19	18	9.5	8.7	8.8	1.38	1.73	1.64
Glass	10	17	17	28.2	38.6	39.4	2.41	2.12	2.12
Metals	118	127	119	66.3	68.5	68.6	3.33	3.60	3.55
Metal products	47	50	43	15.6	15.4	12.9	1.68	1.69	1.67
Mechanical engineering	192	217	213	43.1	40.3	38.2	2.34	2.38	2.29
Instrument engineering	22	24	26	36.8	36.0	36.3	2.36	2.32	2.20
Electrical engineering	146	208	214	55.2	57.5	54.6	2.43	2.56	2.44
Vehicles and aircraft	60	80	86	78.5	80.3	82.8	4.40	5.03	5.38
Shipbuilding	17	13	15	72.5	67.2	76.8	4.64	4.26	3.98
All manufacturing	916	1048	1065	34.5	35.9	36.5	2.58	2.72	2.70

5

The largest industrial corporations

In this chapter we look at the largest industrial companies in the UK and EEC and address ourselves to the following questions:

First, to what extent have the largest companies increased their degree of dominance over the post-war years?

Secondly, what is the composition of the largest group of companies by country and by industry, and how has the composition changed over time?

Thirdly, have there been any noticeable trends in concentration within the largest group of companies?

1 Aggregate concentration in the industrial sector

A marked increase in the degree of dominance of the largest companies seems to have been a feature of many industrial countries over the last ten to twenty years. In the United Kingdom the share of net assets accounted for by the 100 largest industrial and commercial companies increased from 46.5 per cent in 1948 to 63.7 per cent in 1968. As Table 5.1 shows, however, most of this increase occurred after 1957. The sharp increase in the share between 1957 and 1968 coincides with the period of intensified merger activity in the UK and must be explained largely by this factor.

Table 5.1 *Aggregate concentration in the industrial sector, UK 1948, 1957, 1968*

Group of companies	Total net assets as % of all quoted companies		
	1948	1957	1968
10 largest	16.5	18.7	23.7
50 largest	35.0	39.9	50.8
100 largest	46.5	50.7	63.7
All quoted cos.	100.0	100.0	100.0

Sources: National Institute of Economic Research, *Company Income & Finance* 1949–53; *Company Assets and Income in 1957*, HMSO 1960; Department of Trade and Industry. For further comment and definitions see George (1973).

A big increase in aggregate concentration has also been reported for the six original EEC countries over the period of the 1960's. Table 5.2 shows that the largest companies accounted for 35 per cent of the gross product of extractive and manufacturing industries in 1960, and 46 per cent in 1970. The figures in this table are less than satisfactory because while the size of the whole sector is measured by value

Table 5.2 *Aggregate concentration in extractive and manufacturing industries, EEC, 1960, 1965, 1970*

Group of companies	Share of gross product 1960	1965	1970
4 largest	5.8	6.8	8.1
8 largest	10.4	11.8	14.6
20 largest	20.9	22.6	29.0
50 largest	35.1	35.1	45.7

Source: Jacquemin and Cardon de Lichtbuer (1973).

added, the size of the companies is measured in terms of sales which clearly imparts a strong upward bias to the results. However, there can be little doubt that the trend in aggregate concentration in the EEC has been strongly upwards.

The sharp upward trend in aggregate concentration in the UK and other EEC countries has been associated with a high and fast growing level of take-over activity. In the UK average annual expenditure on acquisitions in the industrial and commercial sector was £116m. in 1954–58; £341m. in 1959–63; £810m. in 1964–68; and £1393m. in 1969–72. In relation to gross fixed capital formation the level of merger activity was about four times higher during the last four years of the 1960's as compared to its level in the early years of the 1950's.[1]

In the Netherlands, the number of enterprises acquired or amalgamated in mining, manufacturing and distribution, increased from 100 in the four years 1958–61, to nearly 600 in the four years 1966–69.[2] Again there has been an active merger movement in West German manufacturing industry with major peaks in 1959 and 1970 and another boom year in 1972 in terms of numbers, although not of the value, of acquisitions. Some figures for the UK and West Germany are given in Table 5.3, which appear to show that taking the period 1955 to 1969 as a whole, the level of merger activity has been higher in the UK.[3] This is due largely to the exceptionally high level of UK mergers in the second half of the 1960's which more than offset the higher German level of the late 1950's.

It is also interesting to note that, although the time-distribution of the most intense periods of merger activity does differ, the industrial pattern of merger activity shows a broad similarity between the two countries. The German pattern is shown in Table 5.4. As in the case of the UK, Germany has also experienced its most intense merger activity in such areas as food and drink, engineering, metals, and textiles, leather and clothing. Germany appears to have had more intense merger activity in metal manufacture but of course this is more than offset by the nationalisation of steel in 1967 which does not appear in the UK merger figures.[4]

1 See A. Hughes, *Concentration and Merger Activity in the Quoted Sector of UK Manufacturing Industry*, NEDO, 1973.

2 See H.W. de Jong, *Onderneningsconcentratie*, Leiden, 1971.

3 This conclusion must remain extremely tentative, since German 'joint stock companies' are not the same as 'quoted companies' in the UK and cover a much smaller proportion of the company sector.

4 For further details see K.D. George, The Changing Structure of Competitive Industry, *The Economic Journal* March 1972 (Supplement) K.D. George and A. Silberston, The Causes and Effects of Mergers, *The Scottish Journal of Political Economy* June 1975, and A. Hughes, *Concentration and Merger Activity in the Quoted Sector of UK Manufacturing Industry*, NEDO, 1973.

Table 5.3 *Merger activity in UK and West German manufacturing industry*

Time period	UK Quoted companies acquired as a percentage of total: Number	net assets	West Germany Joint stock companies acquired of merged as a percentage of total: Number	capital stock
	annual averages		annual averages	
1955–58	1.9	0.9	1.4	1.6
1959–63	3.2	1.8	3.2	2.3
1964–69	5.1	3.2	3.0	0.9
1955–69	3.6	2.1	2.6	1.5

Sources: West Germany: Wirtschaft und Statistik
UK: Figures compiled by Mr. A. Hughes of Cambridge University, based on the accounts of public quoted companies

Table 5.4 *Merger activity in West German manufacturing industry*

Industry group	Capital stock of joint-stock companies acquired as percentage of total capital stock in each industry group.		
	1955–58	1959–63	1964–69
	annual averages		
Food, drink and tobacco	5.36	2.67	1.93
Chemicals	0.24	1.16	0.24
Metal manufacture	3.10	5.72	0.85
Mechanical engineering	0.65	1.20	2.10
Electrical engineering	0.69	1.20	2.10
Shipbuilding	0.39	1.09	–
Vehicles and aircraft	–	0.02	0.04
Metal goods	1.38	1.67	1.43
Textiles, leather, clothing	1.78	1.58	1.47
Bricks, pottery, glass, etc.	0.51	1.24	0.54
Wood furniture	0.40	2.09	4.50
Paper, printing, publishing	0.09	4.82	0.71
All manufacturing	1.57	2.29	0.88

Source: Wirtschaft und Statistik

An increase in aggregate concentration together with a high level of merger activity has then been a major feature of EEC economies over the past twenty years. We turn now to the further question of whether there has been any tendency towards increased concentration within the largest group of companies.

2 Concentration amongst the top 100 EEC companies

(a) Introduction

Four basic summary measures of concentration amongst the top 100 EEC companies have been used as well as simply the shares of the top 10, 25, 50 and 75 firms. The four measures are:

(i) *The variance of the log of sales*. This measure has been advocated most notably by Hart and Prais (1956) who argue that the size distribution of companies tends to conform to the log normal, so that a summary measure of dispersion based on this distribution should satisfactorily indicate actual differences in size. However, while their 1956 Royal Statistical Society paper shows that the Lorenz curves derived for particular years over their period behave 'properly' in the sense of not crossing one another, this is not the case for our data. It therefore does not follow that changes in the variance necessarily reflect changes in dispersion at each point of the Lorenz curve. In particular this summary measure does not indicate changes at the top end of the scale.[1]

(ii) *The Pareto Coefficient*. This is defined as Log Sales $= a + b$ Log Rank, and assumes that a Pareto distribution adequately fits the data. Changes in the absolute value of the regression coefficient b (which is negative) indicates changes in the shape of the regression line and hence in the relative size of the larger firms. However, while this equation fits the data very well, the fit becomes progressively worse over the period, and a distinct kink in the curve is evident.

(iii) *The Herfindahl Index*. This is defined as ΣP_i^2, where P_i is the share of the ith firm in total sales. The minimum value of the index (where each firm is of equal size) depends on the number of firms (being the inverse of the number), and the maximum value 1 is obtained when there is only one firm. Since the minimum value depends on the number of firms we have also calculated the relative Herfindahl index (actual as a ratio of the minimum value) for the British and other EEC firms included in the sample. This measure therefore adjusts for differences in the representation of countries over time.

(iv) *Entropy*. This is defined as $\Sigma P_i \log 1/P_i$, where P_i is the share of the ith firm in total sales. The share of each company in total sales is weighted by the logarithm of the reciprocal of the company's share. It is therefore an inverse measure of concentration, falling when concentration increases and rising when a decrease occurs. The value of this measure is again affected by the number of firms in the sample, maximum entropy being given by the log of the number of firms. With one company entropy is zero; with two companies of equal size entropy is one and any subsequent doubling in the number of competitors adds a unit of entropy. In view of this sensitivity of the measure to the number of firms, relative entropy (actual entropy as a percentage of maximum) has been calculated and used as a summary measure of changes in concentration among groups of firms within the top 100.

Identification of the largest companies is based on the 'Fortune' data of the sales of large corporations. The data are not entirely satisfactory in view of a number of factors. In particular, although for most companies only subsidiaries which are more than 50 per cent owned are included in the sales figures, there are some for which subsidiaries less than 50 per cent owned are also included. In addition, although most companies consolidate their sales on a world-wide basis, for some the sales figure refers only to domestic sales. Moreover the sales figures all exclude excise taxes and customs duties, but in some cases Fortune has to estimate the amount of these and subtract them from reported figures. Furthermore, there is no guarantee that all companies which should be in the directory are in fact included. Certain large privately owned concerns are, for example, reluctant to disclose any financial information at all.

1   Doubts about the applicability of the log normal distribution to concentration data have been expressed by several economists, see for instance Silberman (1967), Quandt (1966) and Hannah and Kay (1974).

For our purposes these considerations would not be too important if there was consistency over time. Unfortunately this is not the case. Thus some companies changed the degree of consolidation of their sales figures over the period being analysed, while a few private concerns began to disclose financial details during the period for the first time and are therefore included in the directory as new entrants whereas in reality they should have appeared all the way along.

But clearly we have to use the information available, there being no practical way of improving the series. All we can do is emphasise the qualifications which must inevitably surround the results.

(b) *Changes in concentration 1962 to 1972*

The summary measures of concentration for the 100 largest EEC companies for the eleven years 1962 to 1972 are shown in Table 5.5. Comparing the end years, the variance and Pareto coefficient indicate a rise in concentration, whereas the other three measures shown in the table indicate a decline in concentration. Moreover the former two measures indicate a marked shift in the pattern after 1968, whereas this is not the case with the latter three.

Table 5.5 *Measures of sales concentration among the 100 largest EEC companies, 1962 to 1972*

Year	Variance of log of sales	Pareto Coefficient	Herfindahl Index	Entropy	Relative entropy
1962	0.388	−0.667	0.022	4.274	0.928
1963	0.373	−0.653	0.022	4.285	0.931
1964	0.367	−0.649	0.021	4.299	0.934
1965	0.376	−0.653	0.021	4.302	0.934
1966	0.379	−0.653	0.020	4.314	0.937
1967	0.377	−0.652	0.020	4.309	0.936
1968	0.432	−0.696	0.020	4.295	0.933
1969	0.440	−0.700	0.019	4.305	0.935
1970	0.450	−0.707	0.019	4.309	0.936
1971	0.471	−0.722	0.019	4.299	0.934
1972	0.461	−0.710	0.018	4.316	0.937

Source: Fortune Directory

Table 5.6 *Concentration of sales of the 100 largest EEC companies 1962, 1967, 1968 and 1972*

Number of companies	1962	1967	1968	1972
10	34.1	32.3	32.0	30.3
25	53.8	52.1	54.3	53.1
50	75.5	74.7	76.4	77.5
75	90.0	90.1	90.7	91.2

Source: Fortune Directory

Table 5.6 shows the changes in the shares of the top 10, 25, 50 and 75 companies within the top 100. Over the whole period there was a slight decline in the share of the 25 largest companies and a more marked decline in the share of the top ten. The top 50 companies lost ground in the first half of the period but over the whole period they increased their share by two percentage points. In general, therefore, there has been a tendency for the dispersion of firm sizes within the top 100 companies to decrease, but Table 5.6 well illustrates the problem of devising a measure of concentration which tells us what is happening to relative firm size at every point on the size distribution curve.

Finally, Table 5.7 shows summary measures of concentration applied to UK and other EEC firms, separately, Once again the variance of the log of sales gives a different direction to the change in concentration than do the Herfindahl and entropy measures. As far as the latter are concerned a comparison of 1962 and 1972 indicates a decrease in concentration for both groups of firms. However, the magnitude of the change depends on the allocation of Shell, Unilever and Dunlop-Pirelli. If they are each treated as one company then the results indicate very little change in concentration in the UK, and a decrease in the Rest. This result is consistent with the findings of Jacquemin and Kumps (1971). Their analysis of the top 100 companies over the period 1962 to 1969 shows that the entropy measure for the British firms remains stable, while for the other EEC firms entropy and relative entropy show an increase – i.e. a decrease in concentration. If, on the other hand, – and perhaps more appropriately – these companies are each treated as two companies in the manner indicated by the footnotes to Table 5.7, then the concentration change for the UK and the Rest is very similar – both groups showing a very slight decline in concentration.

Table 5.7 *Measures of sales concentration among the 100 largest UK and other EEC companies 1962 to 1972*

Year	Variance of log of sales UK	Rest	Herfindahl index UK	Rest	Relative entropy UK	Rest	Entropy UK	Rest
1962	0.305	0.422	0.041	0.041	0.936	0.911	3.476	3.716
	(0.389)	(0.356)	(0.042)	(0.028)	(0.925)	(0.944)	(3.478)	(3.850)[a]
1963	0.292	0.404	0.040	0.039	0.939	0.914	3.488	3.728
1964	0.276	0.407	0.037	0.038	0.945	0.917	3.533	3.723
1965	0.284	0.424	0.038	0.037	0.947	0.917	3.493	3.753
1966	0.280	0.409	0.036	0.035	0.948	0.923	3.544	3.749
1967	0.291	0.395	0.036	0.037	0.946	0.922	3.558	3.729
1968	0.403	0.431	0.042	0.035	0.931	0.920	3.410	3.784
1969	0.360	0.459	0.039	0.033	0.938	0.924	3.460	3.783
1970	0.343	0.483	0.041	0.031	0.939	0.926	3.417	3.820
1971	0.359	0.505	0.043	0.031	0.936	0.924	3.381	3.827
1972	0.351	0.466	0.038	0.031	0.940	0.931	3.492	3.795
	(0.399)	(0.420)	(0.038)	(0.025)	(0.933)	(0.948)	(3.509)	(3.899)[b]

Source: Fortune Directory

[a] Counting Shell and Unilever each as two companies and attributing 40% of sales to UK and 60% to the 'Rest'.

[b] Counting Shell and Unilever each as two companies as above and also counting Dunlop-Pirelli as two companies, divided 50/50 between the UK and Italy.

3 Composition of the largest companies by country and industry

Finally we turn to an examination of the composition of the largest companies, first by country and then by industry.

(a) *Composition by country*

The composition of the largest EEC companies by country is shown in Table 5.8.

Amongst the top 150 companies in the EEC the United Kindgom had the highest representation in 1971 with $61\frac{1}{2}$ companies as compared to West Germany's $41\frac{1}{2}$ and France's 28. In the largest size category, however — the 1–50 class — West Germany has 17 companies as compared to the UK's $13\frac{1}{2}$.

Table 5.8 *Largest 150 companies in the EEC in terms of 1971 turnover*

Rank	UK	WG	France	Italy	Neth.	Belg.	Lux.
1 – 50	$13\frac{1}{2}$	17	11	$4\frac{1}{2}$[a]	3[a]	1	0
51 – 100	26	$9\frac{1}{2}$[b]	7	2	2	$2\frac{1}{2}$[b]	1
101 – 150	22	15	10	1	1	1	0
Total	$61\frac{1}{2}$	$41\frac{1}{2}$	28	$7\frac{1}{2}$	6	$4\frac{1}{2}$	1

Sources: Fortune and Vision directories, taking an average of the two and excluding companies not included on both lists. Of the 150 companies 94 are given the same number of employees by both sources. 13 differ substantially.
[a] Including Shell, Unilever (UK–Netherlands) and Dunlop-Pirelli (UK–Italy).
[b] Including Agfa-Gevaert (Germany–Belgium).

Table 5.9 *Representation in top 200 companies outside the US, 1962 and 1971*

Rank	UK 1962	UK 1971	W. Germany 1962	W. Germany 1971	France 1962	France 1971
1 – 50	11	8	15	13	5	9
51 – 100	16	11	8	7	6	5
101 – 150	17	12	5	2	9	4
151 – 200	10	11	8	7	7	6
Total	54	42	36	29	27	24

Source; Fortune Directory

The same results are seen in the wider context of Table 5.9 which gives details of the top 200 companies outside the United States. Here again the UK has the largest number of European companies in the top 200 but West Germany has the highest number in the top 50.

As far as changes in representation over the nine years 1962 to 1971 are concerned, the UK, W. Germany and France have all shown a decline in representation although France has almost doubled its representation in the top 50.

(b) *Composition by industry*

More interesting perhaps than the above comparisons however is the industry breakdown of the largest companies as shown in Table 5.10. The table gives details for the 150 largest companies in the EEC in 1971.

The most striking feature is undoubtedly the dominance of UK companies in the food, drink, tobacco sector and to a lesser extent in textiles, paper and printing and building materials. Thus Table 5.10 shows that in 1971 39 out of the top 150 companies were engaged mainly in these four industrial sectors and that $31\frac{1}{2}$ of these were UK companies. In contrast, the UK is relatively weak in chemicals and metal and metal products as compared to West Germany. In chemicals, only four out of the 23 largest companies in 1971 were British, and out of 36 companies producing

Table 5.10 *Industrial composition of the 150 largest EEC companies, 1971*

Industry sector	Total	UK	WG	France	Italy	Neth.	Belg.	Lux.
Food, drink, tobacco	24	20½	1	2	–	½	–	–
Textiles	4	3	–	1	–	–	–	–
Paper and printing	4	3	–	1	–	–	–	–
Building materials	7	5	–	2	–	–	–	–
Rubber	3	½	1	1	½	–	–	–
Mining	9	4	2	3	–	–	–	–
Vehicles, aircraft	14	4	4	5	1	–	–	–
Electrical engineering	16	7	5	2	1	1	–	–
Oil	8	2½	1	2	1	½	1	–
Chemicals	23	4	9½	4	2	2	1½	–
Metals, metal products	36	8	17	5	1	2	2	1
Other	2	–	1	–	1	–	–	–
Total	150	61½	41½	28	7½	6	4½	1

Sources: Fortune – Vision directories.

metals and metal products only 8 were British. It is interesting to note, however, that this British 'weakness' in these industrial sectors is not so marked within the population of the largest 100 companies. Indeed the left hand columns of Table 5.11 show that as well as being dominant in food, etc., the UK is also well represented, as compared to West Germany, in all other industrial sectors. Metals and metal products is the only sector in which the UK has fewer large companies. It is outside the ranks of the top 100 companies therefore that the number of UK companies in chemicals and metals is markedly lower than in West Germany.

Looking at the changes which have occurred over the ten year period 1962 to 72 it can be seen (Table 5.11) that, within Europe, the UK has maintained its dominance in food, drink and tobacco, textiles, and paper and printing. This has also been true within the wider context of the top 200 companies outside the US except for paper and printing (Table 5.12). On the other hand the representation of large UK companies in the list has declined in vehicles and aircraft, and metals and metal products. This has been due largely to the death of large companies in these fields by merger and nationalisation, and also possibly in part to the slower internal growth of UK companies as compared to overseas competitors.

What explains the existence of so many large firms in the food sector in the UK which is so completely at odds with the situation in the other EEC countries? A number of possible factors spring to mind. First, British companies in this area have undoubtedly enjoyed the advantage of long-standing links with raw material producers in the Commonwealth countries, and the nature of this trade may well have encouraged large-scale organisation.

Secondly, while competition in terms of international trade has not been particularly important in food and related products, nevertheless international competition has by no means been unimportant. In particular it has taken the form of the establishment of subsidiaries of overseas corporations. In the UK there has been intense competition from US companies over a great many years, a feature which has not been so prevalent in other European countries, and this may have promoted greater scale among British enterprises in an attempt to maintain market shares.

Thirdly, food manufacturers in the UK have faced a more concentrated retail trade than their counterparts in the rest of Europe, which means that the balance of

Table 5.11 *Industrial composition of 100 largest EEC companies, 1962 and 1972*

Industry sector	1972 Total	1972 UK	1972 WG	1972 France	1962 Total	1962 UK	1962 WG	1962 France
Food, drink, tobacco	15	13½	1	–	10	9½	–	–
Textiles	3	2	–	–	4	2	–	–
Paper and printing	2	2	–	–	4	3	–	1
Rubber	2	½	–	1	3	1	–	1
Mining	5	2	1	2	3	1	2	–
Vehicles and aircraft	13	4	4	4	16	7	3	5
Electrical engineering	12	5	3	2	11	5	3	1
Oil	8	2½	1	2	6	1½	1	1
Chemicals	12	3	3½	1	10	1	6	2
Metals, metal products	22	5	7	6	31	10	11	6
Other	6	2	1	3	2	1	–	1
Total	100	41½	21½	21	100	42	26	18

Source: Fortune Directory

Table 5.12 *Industrial composition of largest companies in top 200 outside the US: UK, West Germany, and France, 1962 and 1971*

Industry sector	1971 UK	1971 WG	1971 France	1962 UK	1962 WG	1962 France
Food, drink, tobacco	15	–	–	12	1	–
Textiles	2	–	–	2	–	–
Paper and printing	2	–	1	5	–	1
Building materials	1	–	2	3	–	1
Rubber	1	–	1	1	1	1
Mining	4	2	3	2	3	1
Vehicles and aircraft	3	4	4	8	3	7
Electrical engineering	5	4	2	7	4	3
Oil	2	1	2	1	1	3
Chemicals	2	6	4	2	7	3
Metals, metal products	5	12	5	11	16	7
Total	42	29	24	54	36	27

Source: Fortune Directory

bargaining power in the negotiation of trade terms has tended to be tilted more towards distributive organisations in the former than in the latter. This puts a premium on size *per se* as far as producers are concerned if they are to maintain their share of the overall profit margin.

Fourthly, and perhaps most importantly, there undoubtedly exists a marked difference in the pattern of food consumption in the UK as compared with that in Germany, France or Italy. Expenditure in Britain is more heavily concentrated on manufactured or convenience food than is the case in these other countries. Taking bread as an example, sliced, pre-packed loaves account for the major part of the British market whereas such a product hardly exists at all on the Continent. While this may be put down to a difference in tastes the question arises as to the extent to which the marketing techniques of manufacturers has 'forced' consumers into the purchase of convenience foods and reinforced any innate preference which the British have for such items. Certainly it is not implausible to suggest that the demand for food products has not been wholly independent of the actions taken on the supply side. If so, we might anticipate some future change in this direction in other EEC countries as a consequence of manufacturers in the UK – whether British or American – extending their operations on the mainland.

Although the UK has in general been successful in maintaining its representation in the ranks of the largest companies this may have very little relevance to considerations of efficiency and competitiveness.

First, as noted above, British strength within the ranks of the top 100 companies may conceal weakness in the number of companies in lower size-classes.

Secondly, it is likely that the large British firms have had to rely more heavily on take-overs as a means of maintaining their position in the size-hierarchy than has been the case for their continental competitors. This greater reliance on external expansion almost certainly has meant smaller gains in efficiency.

Thirdly, and reinforcing the second point, the figures on which the comparisons are based are the consolidated sales of companies on a world-wide basis. During the 1960's the investments of British companies overseas increased much more rapidly than domestic investment. If, as seems likely, the overseas investments of other European companies in general increased at a slower rate, then the success which British companies have shown in maintaining their representation in the top 100 has been achieved in part by the faster expansion of overseas activities which has not strengthened domestic competitiveness.

Fourthly, UK strength in terms of large firms is biassed towards those sectors which have on the whole been least affected by international competitive forces. This is the case for many products in food, drink and tobacco, paper and printing and building materials. Using the percentage of output exported from the UK and West Germany as an indicator of the strength of international competition, Table 5.13 shows that the sectors in which UK firms tend to dominate in Western Europe have on the whole a relatively low proportion of exports in total output. On the other hand the relative weakness of the UK, particularly in chemicals, metals and

Table 5.13 *Percentage of output exported: UK and West Germany, 1963*

Industry sector	Percentage exports WG	UK
Food, drink, tobacco	1.8	7.1
Textiles	8.4	20.9
Clothing	2.7	7.8
Footwear	3.2	6.5
Wood, furniture	4.5	1.9
Paper	8.1	7.9
Paper products	4.3	4.6
Printing and publishing	1.3	8.7
Rubber and asbestos	12.0	16.9
Chemicals and allied	24.8	19.5
Pottery, etc.	25.8	} 19.2
Glass	14.7	
Metals	18.1	15.0
Metal products	13.4	14.2
Mechanical engineering	27.8	27.1
Scientific instruments	33.6	34.7
Electrical engineering	17.9	19.5
Vehicles and aircraft	32.4	34.1
Shipbuilding	42.5	17.4
All manufacturing	15.4	17.4

engineering, occurs in industries which, as shown by Table 5.13, are greatly exposed to international competition. As we shall argue in Chapter 6 the interaction between growth, investment, and productivity performance involves the growth of demand in world markets not just domestic ones. This dependence on world markets is clearly most important in heavily traded goods, and Britain's failure over the greater part of the 1950's and 1960's to maintain competitiveness in export markets has been a major factor in explaining the weak representation of her companies in these sectors.

6

Changes in output, employment and labour productivity in manufacturing, UK and West Germany

1   Introduction

In the earlier chapters on the size of enterprises and plants some evidence was presented which pointed to the declining competitiveness of British industry. Further research of a more detailed nature is clearly needed. However, to round off this stage of the research it is useful to examine at a highly aggregative level, the performance of UK manufacturing industry in terms of changes in output and productivity, and to make some comparisons with West Germany.

It is a well-known and much-documented fact that the UK has experienced a much slower rate of growth of output and labour productivity in manufacturing since the war than that of virtually all of her main competitors. In this chapter we compare the performance of UK industry groups during this period with the same sectors in West Germany. Our concern is first to pinpoint the main areas of divergence and secondly to look at the relationship between changes in output, employment and labour productivity in the two countries, with the object of seeing whether any significant differences emerge. The analysis is based mainly on data derived from the United Nations, *Growth of World Industry* Volume I, which compiles statistics by two-digit industries – approximately corresponding to industry orders in the UK. Some attempt is made to see whether the results are confirmed at a more disaggregated level by examining the pattern shown by more narrowly defined trades, using Census of Production figures for the UK and series constructed by the Deutsches Institut für Wirtschaft Forschung for West Germany. We begin however by briefly reviewing previous studies of the growth-productivity relationship.

2   Previous studies

Most analyses of labour productivity growth in manufacturing have found a positive association between this and the rate of growth of production.[1] This is so whether

---

[1] Some correlation between changes in output and output per head (or manhours) might be expected since output appears on both sides of the equation, so that if changes in employment were randomly distributed with respect to output some correlation would be likely to emerge. However, it would be surprising if these two variables were independent of each other and to this extent any correlation which emerges is not spurious. The problem can be overcome if the regression is performed directly in terms of employment and output growth. In fact this equation is a 'mirror image' of that of productivity growth on output growth, since the two regression coefficients sum to unity and the two constants to zero if exponential growth rates are taken, the standard errors being the same in both cases.

a sample of industries is taken within a single country or whether the performance of manufacturing is compared as between countries. Moreover it seems to hold no matter what the time period chosen for investigation, though admittedly most work, for data reasons, has been confined to the comparatively recent past. The relationship tends to be closer the longer the period chosen for study, with the correlation coefficient being around 0.8, but even for fairly short runs of years, the coefficient is usually still highly significant. However while the finding is common to a great many studies, the interpretation placed on the relationship in question varies somewhat between investigators. The mere observation of a positive correlation between output and labour productivity changes leaves a good deal of scope for differing views as to the underlying mechanism at work. In itself it tells us nothing about the causal process, or indeed whether this runs from above average increases in output to higher than average rises in output per head or *vice versa*. This can only really be determined by a detailed examination of how gains in labour productivity are actually realised in individual plants or enterprises. However to collect the necessary data in a sufficiently reliable and appropriate form and then to make a satisfactory analysis, which enables general conclusions to be drawn, represents a formidable task to say the least. Most investigators, have in fact stopped well short of this type of study and have been content to rely on what they know of the manufacturing operation in fairly broad terms or on information that is readily available. A few, in addition, have attempted to support their argument by placing the correlation between output and productivity growth in the context of other pertinent relationships, or lack of them, between the two variables and other elements.

Our purpose here is not a systematic review of the research done so far in what is a fairly well-ploughed field, especially in recent years, but, given the relative uniformity of the findings, to pick out the studies which appear to have had the biggest impact and which give a representative picture of those findings. The pioneering work on the association between changes in output and output per head was undertaken by Verdoorn (1949) who lent his name to the law, which according to Kaldor (1966) 'asserts that with a higher rate of growth of output, both productivity and employment increase at a faster rate, the regression coefficients of each being of the same order of magnitude'. In other words, a tendency was found, in a cross-sectional study of industries, for a ten percentage point above average increase in output to be associated with a rise in labour productivity of approximately five percentage points above average and an increase in employment also of about five points above average.

A similar result emerged from Kaldor's analysis of manufacturing performance in 12 'industrially advanced' countries over the period 1953–4 to 1963–4. Countries which experienced the fastest growth of manufacturing output also tended to have the largest rises in labour productivity and labour inputs. Kaldor interpreted this result as evidence for the importance of increasing returns, both in a static and dynamic sense. An increase in the scale of industrial activities gives rise to the realisation of economies of large-scale production and a greater division of labour, which 'generates more skill and know-how . . . (which) in turn yields more innovations and design improvements.'[1] The emphasis is therefore firmly on increases in output leading to gains in productivity and the reverse direction of causation is explicitly

1   See Kaldor (1966) p. 9.

rejected. Thus according to Kaldor, if productivity growth rather than output growth were the autonomous factor, inducing increases in demand by lowering costs and prices, this would not account for 'the large differences (in performance) in the *same* industry over the *same* period in different countries',[1] since each had access to the same improvements in technology. Moreover doubt is cast on whether productivity growth rate variations are likely to be fully reflected in the movement of relative prices and, if so, whether the price elasticity of demand is always greater than unity for the relevant products. Having established the causal process underlying the relationship, Kaldor goes on, first, to demonstrate that Verdoorn's Law is peculiar to the manufacturing sector alone and does not apply to the primary or tertiary sectors, and secondly, to lay stress on the fact that while a higher rate of output growth realises gains in labour productivity, it does not obviate the need for increases in employment.

There are a number of points to which this analysis gives rise.[2] First, although it is not implausible to suggest that advanced countries have more or less equal access to technological improvements, the critical factor here is surely whether each country has the same ability or willingness to apply such improvements to the production process and to tolerate the upheaval which this usually implies, although it is not unlikely that any reluctance to innovate might be overcome by a sufficiently high rate of growth. While a rapid rate of output increase is likely to ease the strain to a great extent, other considerations may well be of some importance. Differences in relative factor prices, for example, might also lend varying degrees of inducement to the introduction of new techniques.

The second point is that a number of studies (e.g. Salter, 1966; Kendrick, 1961; and Nicholson and Gupta, 1960) have in fact found there to be an inverse relationship between both changes in output and changes in labour productivity and price, though admittedly these have been based on inter-industry rather than inter-country comparisons, and Kaldor's second requirement – that price elasticity be greater than unity – has not really been empirically tested.

Thirdly, and perhaps most importantly, Kaldor does not really apply the most appropriate test to check whether increasing returns to labour are a prevalent feature of expansion. As pointed out by Cripps and Tarling (1973) in their more detailed examination of the Kaldorian propositions, the crucial question is whether there is a positive relationship between changes in productivity and *employment*, since the hypothesis is couched in terms of an increase in inputs leading to a more than proportionate increase in output. Those countries showing the largest rises in the manufacturing labour force should also tend to realise the biggest gains in labour productivity if the economies described by Kaldor are important. For the period 1951 to 1965, Cripps and Tarling do in fact find that this is the case, to a certain extent, for the 12 countries included in the Kaldor study. The regression equation is:

$$p_{MF} = 3.178 + 0.549 e_{MF} \quad R^2 = 0.36$$
$$(0.133)$$

---

1 See Kaldor (1966) p. 13. Professor Kaldor's italics.

2 The following section has benefited from a paper written by R.E. Rowthorn of Cambridge University, entitled 'What Remains of Verdoorn's Law?' (1974).

where the dependent and independent variables are respectively productivity and employment growth. The regression coefficient is clearly significantly greater than zero, though the fit is not all that close.[1]

If, however, the observations relating to Japan, which showed by far the highest values for both variables, were to be excluded, the regression coefficient no longer remains significantly greater than zero.[2] The reason for this is that the variation in employment growth between the other 11 countries over this period is insufficient to give a significant association. Moreover the relationship breaks down completely in the period 1965 to 1970 even if Japan is included in the sample. Nevertheless, though clearly not entirely supporting the increasing returns hypothesis, the evidence as yet appears insufficient to be able to discount its validity, as regards inter-country comparisons, with any degree of confidence. Thus, for example, one needs to have a good reason for excluding the Japanese observations from the sample, other than that to do so destroys the significance of the regression coefficient.

As far as inter-industry comparisons within individual countries are concerned, there are firmer grounds for doubting the importance of increasing returns as a primary explanation of variations in labour productivity growth, though they may well be a secondary influence. Very few studies have found a significant relationship between changes in productivity and employment. One major investigator, Salter, did in fact do so, but he tended to play down the result. He argued that any association between the two variables would be the net outcome of two opposing influences: 'first, the direct effect of the possibility of producing the same output with less labour and second, the indirect expansive effect arising out of lower costs'.[3] As this indicates, Salter saw the relationship primarily in terms of the reverse direction of causation as compared with Kaldor – a rapid rate of productivity growth producing a relative decline in cost and price and so stimulating an increase in the demand for the industry's output, partly met, perhaps, by an expansion of its labour force. Thus while a positive association between productivity growth and output growth is predicted, the hypothesis has nothing definite to say about that between the former and changes in employment.

This view, of course, leaves productivity growth unexplained, as Kaldor pointed out, but to Salter, improvements in technical knowledge and in the process of production play the key role here, though the mechanism is regarded as more complex than this might imply. The realisation of economies of scale and factor substitution are also seen as potential elements in the process, all the influences being 'highly interrelated'. To quote 'realisation of economies of scale depends upon increases in output which are in part induced by technical advances; while factor substitution is prompted by changes in relative factor prices which to some extent originate in

1   This equation implies that the regression of output growth on employment growth is:

$$q_{MF} = 3.178 + 1.549 e_{MF} \quad R^2 = 0.82$$
$$\phantom{q_{MF} = 3.178 + }(0.133)$$

The regression coefficient in this case is significantly greater than unity implying that increases in employment tended to be associated with more than proportionate increases in output.

2   The same applies *mutatis mutandis* if output growth is taken as the dependent variable. This result is taken from Rowthorn (1974).

3   See Salter (1966) p. 123.

technical change itself'. These factors are thought of as reducing the costs of the best-practice methods of production in the first instance, which 'leads to an expansion of output and a fall in prices' the latter of which forces 'the abandonment of high-cost obsolete methods.'[1] Labour productivity therefore increases both through the addition of new capacity and through the abandonment of old capacity, industry production becoming concentrated in the most up-to-date plants. An increase in output would tend of itself to produce this latter effect, and in this sense the relationship between the growth in productivity and output embodies a two-way process as regards the direction of causation, though there is little question that Salter regarded technical change as the main autonomous factor and capital investment as the vehicle *via* which such change is implemented.

Of course, it is much more likely that access to, and the adoption of, improvements in techniques varies as between industries over a given period than is the case as between similar industries in different countries, especially with the expansion of multi-national companies. In other words, there seems no clear-cut reason why the explanation of differences in manufacturing performance across countries should be the same as that for those across industries, and to this extent the Salter and Karldorian hypotheses may not be directly conflicting.

Certainly, however, most investigators concerned with inter-industry comparisons have adopted a less extreme view with regard to the direction of causation as between changes in productivity and output than Kaldor, many recognising that the relation could run both ways at the same time. Nevertheless there is some dispute over the predominant mechanism. Thus Caves (1968) regards the negative correlation between output growth and price changes, which emerges from many studies including Salter, but in this case in particular from the Nicholson and Gupta analysis, as the crucial evidence indicating productivity growth as the autonomous variable. His contention that 'if output growth predominantly causes productivity growth, then the selling prices of fast-growing industries should generally be rising, if only to reflect short-run full-utilization of capacity' is however open to debate, since it seems not only to disregard the possibility of increasing returns but to ignore what is happening to prices in slow-growing industries.

In contrast, Kendrick from his analysis of productivity trends in the United States, comes to the conclusion that, 'the significant association between relative changes in productivity and in output is not due just to the influence of productivity on price and therefore on sales . . . increases in output make possible economies of scale that augment autonomous innovation in producing productivity advance. In fact, our analysis suggests that the influence of relative changes in scale on relative productivity changes may be more important than the reverse influence working through relative price changes.'[2]

To sum up, while there is no disputing the widespread tendency for labour productivity growth to be closely associated with the expansion of output, there is still room for debate over the process underlying the correlation. Perhaps the most sensible conclusion is that the direction of causation can run both ways and that there is likely to be some interaction between the two, in the sense that whatever initiates

1   See Salter (1966) p. 143.

2   See Kendrick (1961) p. 209.

the process, changes in one variable will facilitate changes in the other, resulting in a process of 'cumulative causation'. Of course, conditions are especially favourable to exceptional gains in both output and productivity for those products where, due for instance to rising incomes, there is a big increase in demand, and where there are also many opportunities for technological improvements. However, although the evidence supports the view that an increase in manufacturing output generally requires a less than proportionate increase in employment, there are no firm grounds for holding that an increase in employment would necessarily generate a more than proportionate increase in output.

3 The UK performance

Turning specifically to the UK, as we mentioned at the outset, a consistent finding of international studies of productivity growth is that this country has performed much less well than virtually all of her main competitors during the post-war period. Moreover, this has been associated with both a slower rate of growth of manufacturing output and a lower ratio of gross investment to output in the secondary sector. This is demonstrated in Table 6.1, which shows the experience of the UK and nine other advanced countries in terms of these two variables.

Table 6.1 *International comparison of growth and investment in manufacturing, 1960 to 1970*

	Growth of output % p.a.	Gross investment – output ratios
Japan	12.5	30.5
Italy	9.8	n.a.
Netherlands	6.4	18.8
France	6.3	17.4
W. Germany	5.8	15.9
Belgium	5.4	18.7
Canada	4.8	14.5
Denmark	4.7	10.4
US	4.0	11.7
UK	3.1	13.0

Source: OECD *National Accounts of OECD Countries*

As well as the indirect effect which it has on efficiency, gross investment is also an extremely important component of demand for a number of industry groups, as is shown by the industrial input-output table in the 1971 National Income and Expenditure Blue Book. It is particularly important of course for mechanical and electrical engineering and vehicles. For mechanical engineering gross domestic investment accounted in 1968 for 54 per cent of the demand of final buyers and 41 per cent of total output including intermediate output. A period of low investment can clearly have a very damaging effect on the efficiency of a sector of this kind, since it means a low demand for the output of the sector, falling profitability, and thus a weakening of the process of structural change whereby old plants are replaced by new. There is nothing to impede the closure of old plants but low profitability means that there is little inducement, or indeed finance, to invest in new capacity. The long term competitiveness of the industry is therefore weakened. It is interesting to observe that in a recent (pre-entry) study of the consequences of entry into the EEC for different British industries, (Han and Liesner, 1971), mechanical engineering is one of the sectors which, it is thought, will be most adversely affected. While the revival of demand and the consequential increase in output will have some effect in inducing greater investment it is doubtful whether this mechanism alone will be sufficient. When an industry has shown low output and productivity gains for a considerable period of time and has become **uncompetitive** in world markets, private finance may be difficult to attract. In industries such as **machine tools** there is a **strong case**, therefore, both from the point of view of growth and of efficiency, for major government participation in the finance of investment, implying direct intervention in the necessary reorganisation of industry.

4 The UK–West Germany comparison

The relatively poor performance of UK manufacturing in terms of labour productivity growth over the post-war period has by no means been uniform in extent across all industries. This is indicated very clearly if a comparison is made of UK industry groups with the same trades in West Germany. Table 6.2 shows the rate of growth of output and productivity in the two countries for 15 two-digit industries – or industry orders – between the years 1953 and 1969, as derived from United Nations data.

For all 15 groups it is strikingly apparent that the rate of increase in output was substantially less over this period in the UK than in West Germany. In broad terms, however, the pattern of structural change has been very similar in the two countries. The industries in the table are arranged in descending order of their output growth in the UK and it can be seen that their ranking is not very much different for West Germany – the Spearman coefficient of rank correlation is in fact as high as 0.88.

Table 6.2 *Growth rates of output and labour productivity by industry groups, UK and W. Germany, 1953 to 1969 (% p.a. compound)*

Industry group	Output UK	WG	Labour productivity UK	WG
Electrical machinery	5.56	9.80	3.22	3.54
Chemicals	5.49	9.74	4.80	6.20
Printing and publishing	4.27	6.18	2.85	2.92
Paper and paper products	4.08	6.26	2.52	4.39
Rubber products	3.86	6.87	2.46	2.92
Beverages	3.80	6.01	4.61	3.74
Non-electrical machinery	3.08	5.58	1.44	1.90
Other non-metallic mineral products	3.02	5.34	2.92	4.69
Transport equipment	2.70	8.00	2.69	3.16
Food products (exc. beverages)	2.11	4.73	1.53	2.66
Basic metal industries	1.87	5.45	1.81	4.12
Footwear, wearing apparel	1.34	4.94	2.32	2.81
Tobacco	1.31	4.88	1.47	9.73
Textiles	−0.16	4.36	1.77	5.32
Leather and fur products	−1.24	2.25	0.15	3.43
Average for manufacturing	3.21	6.71	2.79	4.21

Source: United Nations, *The Growth of World Industry*

The major difference, at least at this level of aggregation, as we have said, is not in the pattern of change but in the relative magnitudes of the two variables, the average growth rate of output being over twice as high for Germany as for the UK and that of productivity being 50 per cent higher. Of course the table shows only the performance of fairly broad industry groups and this may well conceal differences in the relative pattern of structural change and in improvements in the use of labour for trades within these groups.

Two other points of interest arise from the table.

First, the biggest proportionate differences in productivity growth are, in general, found in those industries with relatively poor output growth rates in both countries, and where in proportionate terms the differences between the output growth performance are greatest. Thus taking the bottom 6 industry groups, in 4 cases the productivity gain in West Germany is at least twice as high as that in the UK and only in one case (Footwear, wearing apparel) does the UK performance come near to the German one. If we compare the productivity performance of the top 6 industry groups on the other hand, the general impression is one of greater similarity between the figures, with 4 out of the top 6 industry groups showing a similar productivity gain. Thus, although the fastest growing industry groups in the UK grew significantly less fast than their counterparts in West Germany, it would appear that the rate of growth was nevertheless high enough to maintain a productivity performance comparable with the average of German trades. On the other hand it might be argued that these industries were the ones most able to apply advances in technical knowledge and at the same time enjoyed a relatively high income-elasticity of demand for their products. Seen in this light the gains in labour productivity made by the relatively slow-growing German industries as compared with the same trades in the UK would be all the more remarkable.

Secondly, and as a reflection of the differences just mentioned, the association between the growth of output and of output per head is much stronger in the UK than in West Germany, the correlation coefficient being +0.82 in the former and virtually zero in the latter. In West Germany, the relatively slow-growing industrial sectors have, by comparison with the UK, achieved a high absolute rate of growth of output. This seems to have enabled the industries concerned to produce a productivity performance similar to the faster growing sectors. Alternatively, the gains in efficiency made by the former trades may have encouraged the relatively large expansion of output, through their effect on relative prices. What the former view might suggest, for example, is that there is a threshold effect in the relationship between the two variables, productivity growth responding to faster growth rates at the lower end of the growth scale but deriving very little extra benefit when growth rates exceed some critical level, though admittedly this is not the only hypothesis consistent with the evidence.

If we turn our attention to changes in employment and relate these to the growth in labour productivity – which we have argued is the strongest test of the increasing returns to labour hypothesis – the correlation coefficient is negligibly low for the UK, and for Germany, although much higher and significant, is of the 'wrong' sign.[1]

1   The regression equation for Germany is:

$p = 5.03 - 0.482e \quad r^2 = 0.48$
(0.140)

where p and e are respectively the exponential rates of growth of output per head and employment for the 15 groups over the period 1953 to 1969.

This suggests that we can discount increasing returns to labour at least as the *predominant* explanation of inter-industry variations in productivity growth as regards both countries over this period. Indeed in the case of West Germany, those industries which experienced below average increases in their labour force made the greatest gains in productivity. However, if we exclude Tobacco, which showed by far the largest fall in employment and by far the largest increase in output per head, the regression coefficient for Germany becomes no longer significantly different from zero. This result is clearly in line with previous inter-industry comparisons as indicated earlier in the chapter.

As a check on these results the same calculations have been made for the period 1958 to 1968. There may indeed be some justification for concentrating attention on this period as the two end years seem more comparable in terms of the underlying economic conditions in the two countries than the alternatives available. Thus it was not until about 1958 that unemployment in West Germany declined to a level similar to that prevailing in the UK. And 1968 seems a more satisfactory year than 1969, in terms of the similarity of labour market conditions, to take as the end of the period.

The results, however, are not greatly altered by taking a different period of time as the basis for comparison. First, Table 6.3 again shows a similar ranking of industries in terms of output growth, the rank correlation coefficient being 0.69. Secondly, industries in respect of which the German productivity growth was most markedly superior to that of the UK again tend to be those which expanded relatively slowly in both countries. Thus if we take the four industries which were amongst the top five in terms of output growth in both countries – i.e. chemicals, electrical machinery, rubber products and beverages – the British productivity performance was actually better on average than that of Germany – the annual rate of increase in productivity being 4.71 per cent as against 4.59 per cent. On the other hand, the four industries which were amongst the slowest growers in both countries – leather and leather products, clothing and footwear, textiles, and basic metals – showed a productivity growth of 4.76 per cent per year in Germany – which is actually higher than the average for the four most rapidly expanding industries – as against 2.27 per cent per year in the UK. Again the correlation between changes in output and labour productivity is much closer for the UK than for Germany – r^2 being 0.63 for the UK and only 0.12 for Germany. Moreover no significant correlation emerges between changes in employment and output per head for either country if Tobacco is excluded from the sample.[1]

Examination of the data for sub-periods does however reveal that in the latter part of the period there is a greater similarity between the two countries in the relationship between changes in output and productivity. The relevant evidence is shown in Table 6.4. The equations indicate that the correlation between the two variables became closer over the time period considered. For the period as a whole and for the early sub-periods the r^2 for the German data is very low and the regression coefficients insignificant. For 1963–69 and 1963–68, however, there is a marked improvement in the goodness of fit for the German data. The values of the regression

[1] Once again, there is a negative association in the case of West Germany, espeically if Tobacco is included in the observations. The correlation coefficient is negligible for the UK.

Table 6.3 *Growth rates of output and labour productivity by industry groups, UK and W. Germany, 1958 to 1968*

(% p.a. compound)

Industry group	Output UK	Output WG	Labour productivity UK	Labour productivity WG
Chemicals	6.50	10.48	6.64	8.01
Electrical machinery	6.03	7.45	4.02	3.44
Other non-metallic mineral products	4.83	5.25	4.28	5.75
Beverages	4.76	6.01	4.77	3.37
Rubber products	4.60	6.09	3.42	3.53
Printing and publishing	4.31	5.56	3.03	3.24
Non electrical machinery	3.89	3.66	2.26	1.46
Paper and paper products	3.57	5.65	2.70	4.85
Food products	2.30	3.76	2.27	3.12
Transport equipment	2.28	6.93	3.02	2.47
Clothing, footwear	2.25	4.14	3.30	3.29
Basic metal industries	2.21	4.40	2.34	4.77
Tobacco	1.19	4.96	1.54	11.27
Textiles	0.69	4.18	2.99	6.54
Leather and Fur products	−0.82	0.82	0.46	4.43
Average for Manufacturing	3.77	5.84	3.58	5.01

Source: United Nations: *The Growth of World Industry*

Table 6.4 *Growth of productivity on growth of output regression results, UK and West Germany, 1953 to 1969*

Period	UK Constant	Regression coefficient	r^2	WG Constant	Regression coefficient	r^2
1953–69	1.13	0.475 (0.092)	0.67	2.89	0.162 (0.171)	0.07
1963–69	1.65	0.567 (0.095)	0.73	3.27	0.418 (0.198)	0.35
1953–68	1.19	0.473 (0.098)	0.64	3.75	0.076 (0.313)	0.01
1953–58	0.65	0.346 (0.067)	0.67	3.96	−0.070 (0.237)	0.01
1958–68	1.04	0.626 (0.133)	0.63	2.74	0.268 (0.210)	0.12
1958–63	0.32	0.670 (0.126)	0.68	2.62	0.100 (0.234)	0.01
1963–68	1.95	0.564 (0.097)	0.72	2.66	0.550 (0.177)	0.45

For the UK the analysis is based on the fifteen two digit industries listed in Tables 6.2 and 6.3. For Germany the tobacco industry is excluded.

coefficients for these two periods are also very similar whereas they diverge markedly in earlier periods.

The closer correlation between changes in output and productivity for German industry in the period after 1963 is confirmed by the analysis on the basis of more narrowly defined industries. The composition of these and the number included were entirely determined by the information we have been able to collect, and both are not the same for the two countries. As regards Germany, the industries cover all manufacturing but are by no means similarly disaggregated. In other words, some correspond to 'industry orders' while others correspond more to Census industries, on the UK method of classification. As regards the UK, the sample consists of those Census industries on which 1970 Census of Production reports were available at the time of carrying out the analysis and on which it is possible to obtain an appropriate wholesale price index to use as a deflator. Thus the UK industries tend to be more narrowly defined than the German industries included, and this may in itself distort the results.

The regression equations summarising the relationship between output growth and productivity growth for these industries are as follows:

UK
1963–68 $p = 21.6 + 0.351q$, $r^2 = 0.32$, $r = 0.56$
         (0.082) $n = 41$

1963–70 $p = 24.8 + 0.386q$ $r^2 = 0.34$, $r = 0.59$
         (0.085) $n = 41$

Germany
1963–68 $p = 22.8 + 0.534q$ $r^2 = 0.32$, $r = 0.56$
         (0.130) $n = 38$

1963–70[1] $p = 29.6 + 0.296q$ $r^2 = 0.21$, $r = 0.46$
            (0.095) $n = 38$

where p and q are respectively the percentage change in productivity and the percentage change in output, both measured in terms of deflated net output changes.

If we compare the above equations with those derived from more aggregated data, the most striking feature is the decline in the goodness of fit with respect to the UK. However, there are a number of points to bear in mind here. In particular, the above equations are based on changes in deflated net output, or value added, as the measure of output changes in order to correspond with the German data, whereas the previous equations, for the UK at least, were based on volume indices (either physical quantities or deflated gross output). Moreover, the UK industries comprising the sample are a rather odd collection, especially in comparison with the German sample, as a perusal of Appendix 6.1 will show. For example, no engineering trades are included mainly because of the non-publication – and indeed non-availability – of suitable price deflators. On the other hand, the collection is no 'odder' than that used by Salter and Reddaway in their two studies. The results reported here for the UK are in fact broadly similar to those of Reddaway which covered 28 industries over the period 1954 to 1963. In that study the correlation coefficient was 0.69 compared to 0.59 for our 41 industries over the period 1963 to 70. At the same time it should be noted that both Reddaway and Salter based their analyses on changes in the volume of gross output as the measure of output changes rather than changes in deflated net output. As mentioned above this may well make some difference to the results.

[1] Excluding for Germany two industries showing 'unusual' relative changes in the two variables between 1963 and 1970 – Tobacco and Leather – produces the equation:

1963 $p = 22.1 + 0.391q$ $r^2 = 0.45$, $r = 0.67$
       (0.075) $n = 36$

Nevertheless the equations formulated on the basis of more disaggregated industries do indicate a close similarity between the UK and Germany with regard to the relationship in question over the period 1963 to 1970. This contrasts with the wide divergence in the results based on more aggregate data for the longer time period since the mid 1950's, but is in line with the greater similarity which was observed, even on the basis of highly aggregated data, for the period since 1963.

Finally, it is important to note that the interaction between growth, investment and productivity performance involves the growth of demand in world markets, not just domestic ones. During the 1950's and most of the 1960's the export performance of the UK was hampered by a fixed and over-valued exchange rate which, as our productivity fell increasingly behind that of our main industrial competitors, meant that the margin of profit on exports was being increasingly squeezed. Over the 1950's and 1960's the countries with the biggest increases in exports also had, in general, the biggest increases in productivity which, given the regime of fixed exchange rates which existed over most of the period, meant that they were more successful in maintaining the profitability of their exporting industries. Of course, it can be equally argued that precisely because of the low margins earned by British manufacturers on exports, they were less able to finance new investment and consequently their productivity performance suffered in relation to, say, German companies whose high profitability generated the funds for high productivity growth. This process can be seen as cumulative, to the extent that relatively high profitability stimulates relatively large gains in efficiency which in turn increase profits, while countries with low profit margins making comparatively small gains in productivity continually fall further behind their competitors. Moreover it should be recognised that higher profitability means greater ability to compete effectively in the widest sense especially in terms of the number and quality of sales outlets and the service provided to customers.

There is little doubt that the competitive position of UK industry has been badly eroded over the post-war years. What needs to be emphasised is that there are essentially two main ways of raising the efficiency of industry, which do not neccessarily go hand in hand, but which tend to reinforce each other when they do. One consists of cutting out the inefficient parts of production, the other of investing in new plant and machinery. For periods in the recent past – in the late 1960's in particular – there are signs that productivity growth in British manufacturing benefited from plant closures and the shedding of surplus labour. However, the problem has been that this was not associated, either at the time or subsequently, with any significant acceleration in investment.

While a low level of gross investment is a long-standing feature of the UK economy, one factor which might have made an important contribution to this state of affairs in recent years is the intensification of merger activity. Thus not only does expenditure on acquiring subsidiaries represent a substitute for expenditure on new capacity as far as any individual company is concerned, but also it often takes a considerable time for the activities of the two companies involved to be satisfactorily rationalised and reorganised. While this is going on it is likely to divert attention away from internal expansion. If we look at the two periods 1967 to 1969 and 1971 to 1973, periods when there was a substantial increase in manufacturing output, we find that the response of manufacturing investment was very much smaller than in previous periods when there were similar increases in output — such as in 1959 to 1960 and 1963 to 1965. The fact that the two periods of sluggish investment response included years of peak merger activity — in 1968 and 1972 — may be more than just coincidence. Of course such casual empiricism ought not, and is not intended, to be a substitute for the detailed analysis which this hypothesis clearly deserves.

Moreover the intensification of merger activity does not appear to have had the effect on average plant size which might have been anticipated especially as economies of scale are often cited as a major justification for such activity. As is indicated by the analysis of Chapter 4, the size of the largest plants in the UK seems to have declined since 1963 not only relative to West Germany but also in absolute terms, though it is as well to bear in mind that employment is being used as a measure of size so that in terms of output the same changes may not have occurred. In addition it may well be that the main benefits of a merger are found in product-specific economies rather than plant-specific ones — that is in terms for instance of longer production runs achieved as a result of rationalisation rather than in terms of larger plants. Here again further research is needed.

What the pattern of experience in the post-war period suggests is that unless growth in the UK is sufficiently high to induce a higher level of gross investment — internal growth of companies as opposed to growth by acquisitions and mergers — there is a danger that this country while it may end up with more efficient industries as compared with the past, will have smaller industries and a still lower level of activity in manufacturing in relation to our main competitors. If our growth performance continues to be unfavourable relative to other EEC countries, then within the enlarged EEC market the position may well be aggravated by a tendency for private investment funds to gravitate more strongly towards the faster growing areas.

Appendix 6.1 *List of industries used in regression analysis   ression analysis*

UK	West Germany
Grain milling	Construction materials
Lubricating oils	Iron production
Pharmaceutical chemicals	Iron and steel casting
Paint	Wire drawing and cold rolling
Soap and detergents	Non-ferrous metals : primary working
Synthetic resins and plastics	Non-ferrous metal foundries
Dyestuffs and pigments	Chemicals
Polishes	Mineral oil products
Photo-chemical materials	Rubber and asbestos
Iron castings	Wood-working and saw mills
Agricultural machinery	Pulp, fibre and paper
Construction and earth moving equipment	Steel and light metal construction
Domestic electric appliances	Mechanical engineering
Tools and implements	Vehicles
Cutlery	Shipbuilding
Metal holloware	Aircraft
Man-made fibres	Electrical engineering
Spinning and doubling	Precision and optical instruments
Woollen and worsted	Secondary transformation of steel
Jute	Iron, tinplate, metal goods
Rope, twine, nets	Pottery
Carpets	Glass
Narrow fabrics	Wood and furniture
Canvas goods and sacks	Sports goods, toys
Asbestos	Paper and fibre products
Leather goods	Printing and publishing
Weather proof outerwear	Plastic products
Men's and boys' outerwear	Leather
Women's and girls' outerwear	Leather products
Footwear	Footwear
Bricks, fireclay, etc.	Textiles
Glass	Clothing
Cement	Grain milling
Furniture	Vegetable oil and margarine
Cardboard boxes, cartons	Sugar
Packaging products of paper	Brewing and malting
Manufactured stationery	Tobacco products
Rubber	Other food and drink
Linoleum and felt	
Brushes and brooms	
Miscellaneous stationers' goods	

List of works cited

Chapter 2

BAIN, J.S., *International Differences in Industrial Structure*, Yale University Press, 1966.
HOROWITZ, I., Employment Concentration in the Common Market: An Entropy Approach, *Journal of the Royal Statistical Society*, Series A, 1970.
PASHIGIAN, P., Market Concentration in the United States and Great Britain, *Journal of Law and Economics*, 1968.
PHLIPS, L., *Effects of Industrial Concentration : A Cross-Section Analysis for the Common Market*, North Holland, 1971.
PRYOR, F.L., An International Comparison of Concentration Ratios, *Review of Economics and Statistics*, May 1972 (1972a).
PRYOR, F.L., Size of Production Establishments in Manufacturing, *Economic Journal*, June 1972 (1972b).
RAY, G.F., The Size of Plant : A Comparison, *National Institute Economic Review*, November 1966.
SARGANT FLORENCE, P., *The Logic of British and American Industry*, Routledge and Kegan Paul, 1953.
SAWYER, M.C., Concentration in British Manufacturing Industry, *Oxford Economic Papers*, November 1971.
SCHERER, F.M., The Determinants of Industrial Plant Sizes in Six Nations, *Review of Economics and Statistics*, May 1973.
SHEPHERD, W.G., Structure and Behaviour in British Industries with US Comparisons, *Journal of Industrial Economics*, November, 1972.

Chapter 3

ANDREWS, P.W.S., *On Competition in Economic Theory*, Macmillan, 1964.
SAWYER, M.C., Concentration in British Manufacturing Industry, *Oxford Economic Papers*, November 1971.

Chapter 4

ARMSTRONG, A. and SILBERSTON, Z.A., Size of Plant, Size of Enterprise and Concentration in British Manufacturing Industry, 1935–58, *Journal of the Royal Statistical Society*, 1965.
RAY, G.F., The Size of Plant : A Comparison, *National Institute Economic Review*, November 1966.

Chapter 5

GEORGE, K.D., The Changing Structure of Competitive Industry, *The Economic Journal*, March 1972 (Supplement).
GEORGE, K.D., The Changing Structure of Industry in the United Kingdom, in T.M. Rybczynski (ed) *A New Era in Competition*, 1973.

GEORGE, K.D. and SILBERSTON, A.Z., The Causes and Effects of Mergers, *Scottish Journal of Political Economy*, June 1975.
HANNAH, L. and KAY, J.A., *Mergers and Concentration in the UK. 1919–1969*. mimeo.
HART, P.E. and PRAIS, S.J., The Analysis of Business Concentration : A Statistical Approach, *Journal of the Royal Statistical Society*, 1956.
HUGHES, A., *Concentration and Merger Activity in the Quoted Sector of UK Manufacturing Industry*, NEDO, 1973.
JACQUEMIN, A. and CARDON de LICHTBUER, M., Size, Structure, Stability and Performance of the Largest British and EEC Firms, *European Economic Review*, December 1973.
JACQUEMIN, A. and KUMPS, A.M., Changes in the Size Structure of the Largest European Firms : An Entropy Measure, *Journal of Industrial Economics*, November 1971.
de JONG, H.W., *Onderneningsconcentratie*, Leiden, 1971.
QUANDT, R.E., On the Size Distribution of Firms, *American Economic Review*, June 1966.
SILBERMAN, I.H., On Lognormality as a Summary Measure of Concentration, *American Economic Review*, September 1967.

Chapter 6

CAVES, R.E., Market Organization, Performance, Public Policy in R.E. Caves and Associates, *Britain's Economic Prospects*, Allen and Unwin, 1968.
CRIPPS, T.F. and TARLING, R.J., *Growth in Advanced Capitalist Economies 1950–1970*, Cambridge University Press, 1973.
HAN, S.S. and LIESNER, H.H., *Britain and the Common Market: The effect of Entry on the Pattern of Manufacturing Production*, (Cambridge University Press, 1971).
KALDOR, N., *Causes of the Slow Rate of Economic Growth of the United Kingdom, An Inaugural Lecture*, Cambridge University Press, 1966.
KENDRICK, J.W., *Productivity Trends in the United States*, Princeton University Press, 1961.
NICHOLSON, R.J. and GUPTA, S., Output and Productivity Changes in British Manufacturing Industry, 1948–54, *Journal of the Royal Statistical Society*, Series A, Vol. 123, pp. 427–59.
ROWTHORN, R.E., What Remains of Verdoorn's Law? Cambridge mimeo 1974.
SALTER, W.E.G., *Productivity and Technical Change*, Cambridge University Press, 2nd edn. with Addendum by W.B. Reddaway, 1966.
VERDOORN, P.J., 'Fattori che regolano lo sviluppo della produttivita del lavoro', *L'Industria*, 1949.

DATE DUE

DEC 04 1985			
DEC 12 1990			
SEP 04 1991			
APR 22 1992			

DEMCO 38-297

643 .27 LAM
La Mar, Frank J.
Condominiums : The pros
and cons of ownership /

Condominiums
The Pros and Cons of Ownership

Frank J. La Mar

PALM BEACH COUNTY
LIBRARY SYSTEM
3650 SUMMIT BLVD.
WEST PALM BEACH, FL 33406

**Windstorm Creative
Full Spectrum Information Library
Port Orchard 📖 Seattle 📖 Tahuya**

Condominiums: The Pros and Cons of Ownership
copyright 2005 by Frank J. La Mar
published by Windstorm Creative

ISBN 1-59092-036-8
First Edition September 2005
9 8 7 6 5 4 3 2

Cover by Buster Blue of Blue Artisans Design.
Additional fact-checking provided by Benjamin Frances.

All rights reserved, including the right to reproduce this book or portions thereof in any form whatsoever, except in the case of short excerpts for use in reviews of the book. Printed in the United States of America.

For information about hardback, reprint, film or other subsidiary rights, contact Mari Garcia at mgarcia@windstormcreative.com.

Windstorm Creative is a multiple division, international organization involved in publishing books in all genres, including electronic publications; producing games, videos and audio cassettes as well as producing theatre, film and visual arts events. The wind with the flame center was designed by Buster Blue of Blue Artisans Design and is a trademark of Windstorm Creative.

Windstorm Creative
Post Office Box 28
Port Orchard, WA 98366
condo@windstormcreative.com
www.windstormcreative.com
360-769-7174 ph.fx

Windstorm Creative is a member of the Orchard Creative Group, Ltd.

Library of Congress Cataloging-in-Publication Data available.

Dedication

This guide is dedicated to my son, who with infinite patience instructed me in the ways of computer utilization, and to my wife for her never-ending encouragement and emotional support.

Finally, this brief treatise would not have taken shape without the technical expertise of the personnel at Windstorm Creative.

Acknowledgments

Thank you to all the wonderful families I have worked with over the years and to the staff at Windstorm Creative for making this book possible.

Contents

	Foreword	11
Chapter 1:	Definition of a Condominium	13
Chapter 2:	Design and Structure of Condominiums	15
Chapter 3:	Governance	17
Chapter 4:	Amenities	21
Chapter 5:	Living Expenses	25
Chapter 6:	Marketability	27
Chapter 7:	Condominiums as an Investment	31
	Fantasy Living	33
Chapter 8:	Planned Unit Developments	35
Chapter 9:	Conclusions	37
	Appendix A: Declaration	41
	Appendix B: By-Laws	65
	Appendix C: Condominium Rules	79
	Exhibit A: Unit Number & Location	85
	Exhibit B: Unit Value	90
	Exhibit C: Garage Unit Value	92

Condominiums
The Pros and Cons of Ownership

Frank J. La Mar

Foreword

It has rained for three days. The grass around the house looks like a wetland and there are leaves everywhere. You know that into each life some rain must fall, but this was a deluge! To further aggravate your frustration, you suspect that both the mower and the blower will deny you an easy start. Suddenly (it seems) these routine chores have become a personal challenge.

The idea comes to you that some people live without these hassles — in a condominium! Would this change of domicile give you a carefree lifestyle within a secure environment as heralded by condo aficionados? What trade-offs will be mandatory? Will they be acceptable to you?

The impartial review that follows provides the pros and cons of condo living, and should help you reach an *informed* decision. We all know that purchasing a home is usually one of the largest if not *the* largest expenditure we ever lay out.

Developers and realtors respect you as a competent adult who has thoroughly researched all options before approaching them about a condo. Reading this book will ensure that you are indeed informed, ready to work with a seller, and protected against the most common unpleasant surprises that *uninformed* buyers experience as they move from a private home (or apartment) into the communal living of a condominium.

Chapter 1
Definition of a Condominium

A condominium, commonly abbreviated as "condo," is defined as a building consisting of multiple units where each unit is individually owned; each owner receives a deed to the unit purchased. Owners are vested with the rights to rent, mortgage or sell their unit and may share in joint ownership of any common areas and amenities contained within the building or on the property.

As we discuss the pros and cons of condo living, you must never forget that when you purchase a unit you join with the other owners to form a Condominium Association which will influence your freedom of action (more about this later).

For clarity, when the expression "condo complex" or "complex" is used, it refers to the aggregate project. "Condo unit" or "unit" will denote a single unit in the complex.

Chapter 2
Design and Structure of Condominiums

We are all concerned about the configuration and location of a home we are considering to purchase. In this regard, you are sure to find condo units both large and small, "flat" (one story) or up-and-down, in cities and suburbs, new and old, originals and conversions of apartment buildings, high rise and house-like, with or without a garage.

Where acreage exists in suburbs, developers will sometimes build single-level homes attached in groups of two, three or more. By appearance these are more house-like. These units may be called "villas" or "townhouses." Whatever the arrangement, all elements of a Condominium Association will still apply.

The most prevalent condo unit is a two bedroom, two bath standard, possibly located in one large building with forty to fifty other units. Obviously these units are unsuitable for growing families with several children. As condo complexes have become more popular, developers have attempted to reach a greater market by building larger units of three or more bedrooms. Condo units range in size from as small as nine hundred square feet to huge penthouse units which encompass areas larger than many private homes.

In western Washington State, our test area used for this book, attractive two bedroom units can be purchased for roughly $190,000. Three bedroom units usually start at $310,000. There are other areas of the country where real estate is less expensive, but there still exists that premium price for the third bedroom.

The design and size of the living room, dining room, kitchen and bathrooms vary widely with the purchase price. Some living and dining rooms are not separated. In larger units, there is an eat-in kitchen and a separate dining and living room. Bathrooms may be elegant or functional. Should climate control be important to you, even in a temperate area of the country, complexes *do* exist with central air conditioning.

Multi-story complexes usually have elevators. Building codes vary by locality, however, and the criteria for mandating elevators in some areas may permit a strenuous stair climb of several floors. A prospective purchaser who is infirm or elderly should consider only those complexes that offer elevator service.

Of paramount importance is the quality and condition of the overall structure which houses the individual units. Poor construction or delayed maintenance can bring many costly surprises (assessments) to unsuspecting buyers.

My wife and I once bought into a complex which required an immediate $35,000 roof repair. We hadn't been informed of this until the first owners' meeting! We also learned far too late that each owner would have to contribute to pay for it.

Chapter 3
Governance

When you purchase a condo unit, you become a partner with all the other unit owners in your complex. This is a legal entity known as an Association.

In most states, developers must pursue prescribed procedures to declare the formation of a proposed condominium complex (see Appendix A). When the majority of the units have sold, the builder relinquishes responsibility for further administration to the Association.

At that time, the owners must elect a volunteer Board of Directors (BOD), usually made up of five or more members, to manage all central functions essential to the orderly conduct of the Association. Among many other things, the BOD is responsible for:

- Selecting a Treasurer and Secretary for the Association,
- Presiding at owners' meetings,
- Paying Association bills,
- Entering into maintenance, security and insurance contracts,
- Preparing and monitoring operating budgets,
- Maintaining financial accounting either in-house or by contract, and
- Functioning as an information center for owners' concerns and complaints.

18 Condominiums

The BOD provides administrative support for the maintenance, operation, security and general well-being of the Association. It is crucial that BOD members be highly motivated and *willing to grapple with the myriad of opinions and diverse behavior of residents* in the complex.

There are many professional management consultant firms who offer guidance, provide accounting services and assist in the preparation of budget and reserve accounts for an annual fee. The Communities Association Institute is a valuable, national resource organization that provides books, periodicals, educational seminars and advice for Condominium Associations who are enrolled with them. Ultimately, however, the BOD is still responsible to all members for the development and implementation of sound management practices.

Terms of BOD members are prescribed by the Bylaws (see Appendix B). In complexes with passive unit owners, it can become a major problem to induce volunteers to serve.

State laws, Association Bylaws and House Rules (see Appendix C) are a daily reality of condominium living. If, by nature, you chafe under restrictions affecting your lifestyle, condo living is *not* for you.

Here are some examples:

- Most owners may only keep small pets
- You are only as secure as the manager's pass key (all units must be available for pass key entry in an emergency)
- Pool use, if available, is restricted by House Rules

- Recreation rooms must be reserved in advance
- Insurance, such as earthquake or flood, for the entire complex is a BOD decision
- All window coverings must usually be the same for the entire complex
- You may not exhibit signs on the premises such as "Garage Sale," "For Sale," "For Rent," etc.
- Regardless or your judgment concerning Association expenditures, you *must* pay your monthly dues without exception

Chapter 4
Amenities

Some complexes are huge, vertical structures of one hundred units or more, which lure prospective buyers by providing all the amenities you might discover in an elegant hotel (with the exception of room service). There may be valet parking, swimming pools, saunas, spas, exercise rooms, a golf course, tennis courts, twenty-four hour security, an in-house maintenance staff, conference facilities, boutique shops and last, but not least, a full-time on-site manager.

As you might expect, monthly dues in such complexes may range from $500 to $1000 or more per month. In some instances, additional fees are required to use special facilities - especially tennis courts, golf courses and conference rooms.

As I've mentioned before, the majority of the complexes may contain forty to fifty units, and provide minimal basic accommodations such as a central recreation or conference room. This isn't altogether bad. The fewer the amenities, the lower the monthly dues you will pay.

Regardless of which type of complex you consider, the following amenities normally found in a private residence will *not* be available to you:

- Hobby space
- Workshop space
- Garden
- Extensive storage
- Private garage (except townhouses and villas)

Condominiums

Condo living *does* provide freedom from outside chores. The Association's responsibilities include lawn maintenance, exterior building repair, exterior painting, window washing and plumbing repairs up to the point of entry into your unit.

The degree of success achieved in promoting a first class appearance both inside and outside the structure depends on the development of the financial reserves which support timely maintenance and up-grading of the complex.

Common misconceptions of condo living include:

- Many eyes and ears mean greater security
- Families within a complex will feel a common bond, promoting easier social interaction

No one can accurately predict how any random group of people will interact. However, there exists widespread anecdotal evidence which casts an element of doubt on the assumptions listed above.

For example, high-rise condos have remote front entrance opening mechanisms in each unit which allow seemingly polite but ultimately careless residents to let unidentified people into the main lobby without video verification. Police agencies concur that security in condo complexes is no better than in a secure single family dwelling. When responding to an emergency in a single family home, police can easily surround it and identify the perpetrator. Both of these actions are very difficult in multiple family dwellings.

Realistically, no one really knows who should and should not be walking through the complex. Strangers are often believed to be guests. Too often the sense of security you believe in is false, for few people want to get involved. Police records contain the sordid details of a burglary where locked doors have been totally demolished as occupants of adjacent units were either not home or just neglected to respond to the commotion.

We have all been exposed to stories describing how adjacent apartment dwellers go through life never meeting each other and how lonely it can sometimes be to live in isolation, even though you are surrounded by people in a big city. Such was the case that we found when living in a condo complex.

Despite our efforts to reach out, we found other owners resisted close friendships. New friendships will not necessarily abound simply because you live in a condo. Perhaps this is because of the added stress of the owner-populated governing body of the complex or of the owner-funded cooperative for maintenance and repairs (assessments) that take some owners by surprise and foster resentments unless all owners pay promptly and responsibly.

Both of these issues are discussed in detail as we continue.

Chapter 5
Living Expenses

There is no free lunch. This is certainly the truth regarding the benefits derived from condo living. All the inside-the-home expenses that you incur in a single family home or apartment apply to a condo unit as well.

These include telephone, electricity, gas, plumbing repairs, fixture repairs and replacement, painting and appliance repair or replacement, as well as mortgage and real estate taxes.

One of the most costly, repetitive condo expenses is the assessment levied on each unit, which may be called by many different names, but remains a fee you must pay either monthly or in advance. This assessment supports the operation of the Condominium Association. Each unit owner pays a percentage of the total requirement based upon the *original declared* value of the unit owned. The developer has discretionary power when assigning this *original declared* value. Their decision will consider values such as unit view, floor level, and equivalent existing pricing in the marketplace. Once the declaration of value has been established, you can calculate your monthly fee as follows:

Total Declared Value of Complex — $4,000,000
Developer's Declared Value of Unit — $100,000
$100,000 divided by $4,000,000 = .025 or 2.5%

In this example, you and all other similarly valued units would be required to pay a monthly assessment equal to 2.5% of the total needed. Typically this could be $200 or more based upon the extent of amenities and the cost of operations for the entire complex.

    If an unexpected emergency occurs which cannot be funded from available reserves, the BOD will levy a special assessment and you would be required to remit 2.5% of the total needed. When all owners are in good standing with their monthly dues, the Association can meet its obligations. Delinquent owners can create serious operating problems because remedy at law is difficult to enforce payment. Court ordered liens may be placed on deficient units but this does not resolve the immediate shortfall of funds.

Chapter 6
Marketability

While it might be unusual to dwell upon selling when you're busy buying, being confident that any sale in the future will recoup your investment plus a factor of appreciation will minimize the natural buyer's remorse which can follow a large expenditure.

Condos are special real estate; at present time, by and large, there are fewer condo buyers in the marketplace than buyers of single family dwellings. Segments of the country seem to experience cycles of acceptance or rejection of the condo lifestyle. However, medium price units in quality buildings with prime location almost always market successfully.

Many factors, not the least of which is the prevailing economy of the complex's location, will affect how quickly and at what price your unit will sell.

There is no doubt that in the '90s the construction of complexes had accelerated, reflecting widespread acceptance of this way of life. In our hometown, developers often reported that thirty, forty or fifty percent of their units were sold before the foundation was ever laid.

We once owned an elegant two bedroom, two bath unit with imported marble throughout in an all-brick, well-maintained building that was nestled bay-side overlooking a panoramic skyline. Great, right? We grew restless, though, and wanted to go back into a private home.

With mixed feelings we listed with a realtor. People

came... people saw... but no offers were tendered. As the months rolled by, my wife became anxious to seek out a prospective new home. We jousted about this daily. Deep down I knew that if she fell in love with a new home, our price resolve on the condo unit would vanish. We were now two years into a continuous sales effort, and other units in our neighborhood (some right in our complex) were selling at a comparable price. I had to know why our professionally designed and decorated unit had not garnered even a single offer.

One day, we stayed put during an open house. We carefully watched and finally approached a couple who seemed to display some interest. We identified ourselves as the owners and convinced them to give us their gut appraisal of the unit. Reluctantly, they told us their two prime misgivings.

First, they said that although all the lights were on, the unit was dark. It had too little natural light. A condo unit rarely has more than one exterior side with windows. Even though our unit was an end unit with two exterior sides, the light quality could not compare with the many single family homes buyers had seen before. It is a fact that many condo units not only have just one exterior side but that those windows usually face a canopied deck.

The second misgiving the couple had was that the unit was on the first floor. When you become acquainted with condo unit prices, you will invariably discover, all else being equal, the higher the floor the more valuable the unit. Although our complex had garage stalls on the street level and we were set above them, we were still considered first floor. This was how we learned that most buyers feel first floor accommodations are less desirable. Their reasoning includes factors of view, security and noise avoidance.

So there we were, with a unique property, without a buyer for what seemed to be an interminably long and frustrating period. Interestingly, our unit had a refined Asian motif and we were eventually saved by the appeal the unit had on a Japanese-American business man.

Chapter 7
Condominiums
as an Investment

While a majority of condo buyers live in them, there is also an investment factor which may be pursued either short term, for future occupancy, or as a long term asset within an investment portfolio.

As an investment, factors such as appreciation, depreciation, income and operating expenses must be optimized. Once again, depending on geographical location, you must carefully consider market conditions as you attempt to compute a favorable return on your investment. In many areas of the country, real estate prices have suddenly climbed, while rents have *not* kept pace. If you are unable to offset condo unit ownership costs with your rental income made from the unit, you will suffer a *negative* cash flow.

If you get excited by the thought of real estate investing in condo units with the dual benefits of profit and vacationing there, destination resort complexes are very popular.

Condo complexes in Sun Valley, Idaho, Raton, Florida and Aspen, Colorado, are a few examples of the resort complex classification, cited primarily for geographical diversity.

The older, well-established resorts command higher prices than the new and more obscure destinations. Real estate prices do run in cycles and even a nationally known resort like Sun Valley had some excellent investment opportunities when the market there took a dip.

When you own a unit in a resort complex, you again become a partner in the Association. As transients rent these units, you share in the net income after all expenses are satisfied. These units are also directed by the owners' BOD and invariably have an on-site manager who accepts reservations, collects revenue, greets guests and directs the housekeeping staff.

Unlike a complex where you might live year-round, this arrangement is considered a business enterprise. You therefore can declare such business deductions as depreciation, real estate taxes and loan expense on your taxes. In accordance with existing IRS regulations, you can personally occupy your own unit up to fourteen days a year without jeopardizing your business deductions. In many instances, resort units yield a very favorable return on the investment. Many resort condo complexes have bylaws which permit owners a limited stay at *greatly reduced rates.*

So far we have discussed buying, living in and selling a condo unit. We have touched upon the basic facts, such as how a Condominium Association is created by statute and managed by a central authority (BOD) which is elected by the owners. However, there are other forms of unit ownership where the Home Ownership Association provides most exterior chores (by contract) yet imposes minimal living restrictions on the homeowner. The following section outlines two such umbrella associations.

Chapter 8
Fantasy Living

Like the proverbial Shangri-La, several developers across the United States have built large, planned communities which cater to most every leisure activity we know today. These communities are created to provide chore-free living and an environment which lures even shy residents to participate in hobbies, arts and crafts, sports and other social activities.

It would be impossible, except for the very wealthy, to privately duplicate the investment contained in these communities which is solely for the enjoyment of its members. These communities are mostly private single-family homes that are interspersed with villas and townhouses. As a private homeowner, for a modest fee, all the facilities and activities of the community are available to you.

I have visited three of these communities in Florida, Arizona and California, all created by nationally-known builder Dell Webb. I found these impeccably clean communities almost surreal. The residents were busy, good-natured people with an exuberance to share their good fortune with visitors.

Why don't more people live in these idyllic communities? Because the geographic areas available are limited. While more of these communities are constantly being built, they do tend to crop up in typically desert-like locales where land is inexpensive and the weather permits year-round outdoor activities. Additionally, these planned communities very often require buyers (at least one head of the family) to be fifty-five years of age or older.

A fascinating statement about our culture and how we see each other and define maturity, no doubt.

Chapter 10
Planned Unit Developments

If it is only landscape chores that stand between you and a peaceful mind, you may wish to investigate a relatively rare form of home ownership contained in a Planned Unit Development (PUD). The homes are single-family dwellings and are not linked in any way. You own the home and the land it sits on.

For a monthly fee, all yard maintenance is accomplished under contract. This maintenance includes weeding, mulching, pruning, mowing, fertilizing and irrigation. PUDs do not include interior or exterior house maintenance. If you take pride in your community, PUDs will provide the ambiance you seek.

With the PUD comes Covenants, Conditions and Restrictions (CC&Rs). The CC&Rs are common sense rules which discourage unseemly behavior affecting the desirability of the neighborhood, such as disassembled or disabled cars left on the property, owning (or rather parking) commercial trucks, installing large roof-top antennae, etc.

Conclusions

If you are considering buying a condo unit to live in, remember all complexes have an Owners' Association which functions as a governing agency. Buying into a condo automatically makes you a member of the Association with its obligatory monthly dues. The Board of Directors will make rules and decisions which will affect your domicile. Only some of these outcomes will be put to vote where the majority rule will carry.

Upon deliberation, should the condo concept be appealing to you, close scrutiny of the inner workings pertaining to the selected condo complex should be pursued.

You are entitled, *before you buy*, to review the unit and the complex's original declaration, bylaws, house rules and minutes of recent BOD meetings. As you will become part responsible for future financial shortfalls, you or your representative should be satisfied that all financial requirements, especially those in the Reserve Account, are adequate for replacement liabilities. The older the complex, the larger the reserves needed.

You can request a copy of the complex's Replacement Schedule to determine the soundness of the projections in relation to the age of the condo. The Replacement Schedule is the blueprint that indicates whether or not appropriate reserves for replacements and upgrading have been financed in the Reserve Account.

Although you will be only one of many units,

association insurance coverage bears directly on your ability to exist after a major catastrophe. Based on market values, you need to be convinced that the association insurance coverage is adequate. You will only have minimum influence to increase, change or add coverage once you are an owner.

We once owned a unit in a complex which became the tragic scene of an accidental death. Police investigation found that willful misconduct by the deceased had caused the accident. Therefore, the complex was declared blameless. However, it could have been a financial disaster for all the owners if the ruling had held the complex culpable. Make certain that any complex you are about to buy into is free from pending lawsuits and adequately insured against unforeseen catastrophes.

An interesting statistic we have always noted when evaluating a condo complex is the percentage of units therein which are rented rather than owned. If twenty to thirty percent of the units are occupied by renters, it will indicate two things: For some reason the owners of those units would rather be living elsewhere, and you will be dealing with renters who do not have the same concerns as owners and may be more difficult to live with.

Last but not least, if loan money is needed to buy a unit, some banks will decline the mortgage if the percentage of rentals exceeds their loan criteria.

Finally, for long term peace of mind with no regrets, aggressively research the records kept by the complex to determine if all is well (and well-managed) within the Association. If you can't or don't feel comfortable doing this yourself, retain a competent real estate attorney or buyer's agent to assist you.

Now you know what life is like behind the closed doors of a Condominium Association. By being an informed buyer you can determine if condominium living is right for you.

Appendix A
Declaration

Declaration of a Condominium for Camelot Court

John Q. Developer, hereinafter called the "Developer," hereby makes this declaration for the purpose of submitting that certain real property hereinafter described to the provisions of the Maryland Condominium Act of 1983 as amended, hereinafter called the "Act."

Section One
Legal Description

The real property on which the building and improvements hereinafter described is located in Talbot County, Maryland, more particularly described as:

Lots 50, 51, 52 and 53, all in block 54 of 3rd plat of Easton Land and Improvement Company of Easton, according to plat recorded in Talbot County, Maryland; and

Lots 54, 55, 56, 57, 58, 59, 60, 65, 66, 67 and 68 in block 65, replat of Easton Land and Improvement Company's third plat. According to plat recorded in volume 8 of plats, page 68, in Talbot County, Maryland; and

Lots 55, 56, 57, 58, 59, 60, 61, 62, 63 and 64 in block 458 of Easton Tide Lands, hereinafter called the "Site."

Section Two
Description of Building

The condo building located on the Site will consist of two five story buildings denominated as the 'north' and the 'south' buildings. The buildings will each contain twenty residence condos, and there will be forty garage units. The surface level of each building shall contain the garage units, entryways and storage areas. The residence condos commence on the second level and continue through the fifth and these levels are denominated floors 'first' through 'fourth.' The building will be of reinforced concrete and wood frame construction. As used herein the term 'property' shall include the condo buildings and the Site and the improvements thereon.

Section Three
Condo Number and Description

The number of each residence condo, its location, approximate area, number of rooms and immediate common area to which it has access are set forth on Exhibit "A" which is by this reference made part hereof.

The number of each garage apartment and its approximate area are set forth on Exhibit "A".

Section Four
Description of Common Areas

The common areas and facilities shall be those areas and facilities as defined in the Act, all areas not expressly described as part of the individual residence condos and garage apartments or as a limited common area, and including the following:

A) The Site,

B) The concrete foundations, columns, girders, beams, supports, main walls (excluding non-bearing interior partitions of condos), and all other structural parts and roofs of the building,

C) The elevators and elevator shafts, the hallways, and the stairway landings and stairways,

D) The driving areas and the driveways related thereto,

E) The landscaped areas and walkways which surround and provide access to the condo buildings,

F) Storage and parking areas not within or assigned to any condo, the outdoor recreation area and swimming pool, the sauna rooms, the recreation room, the boiler rooms, transformer vault and meter room,

G) Each condo owner shall have the right to permit a mortgagee or deed of trust beneficiary, hereinafter separately and collectively called "Security Holder", covering his condo, or such Security Holder's agents, the opportunity to inspect the common areas at reasonable times and after reasonable notice.

Section Five
Description of Limited Common Areas and Facilities
The limited common areas and facilities consist of:

A) The land adjacent to each residence condo is reserved for the exclusive use of the condo through which access is gained to it.

B) The storage lockers, each of which bears a number similar to a residence condo, shall be for the exclusive use of that condo.

Section Six
Value and Percentage of Undivided Interest in Common Areas

A) The value of the entire property is $5,833,000.00.

B) The value of each residence condo and the percentage of undivided interest in the common areas and facilities appertaining thereto and the limited common areas reserved thereto for all purposes are set forth on Exhibit "B" which is by this reference made a part hereof.

C) The value of each garage apartment and the percentage of undivided interest in the common areas attached to each garage apartment and its owner for all purposes is set forth on Exhibit "C" which is by this reference made a part hereof.

Section Seven
Voting

A) The total voting power of all owners shall be 100 votes, and the total number of votes available to the owners of any one apartment shall be equal to the percentage of undivided interest in the residence apartment and the garage apartment as set forth in Exhibits "B" and "C".

B) All of the owners of condo units shall constitute the Association of Owners as defined in the Act, hereinafter called "Association".

C) There shall be one (1) voting owner of each condo. The voting owner shall be designated by the owner or owners of each condo by written notice to the Board and need not be an owner. The designation shall be revocable at any time by actual notice to the Board of the death or judicially declared incompetence of any owner of the condo or by written notice to the Board by any owner of the condo. Such powers of designation and revocation shall be exercised by the guardian, administrators or executor of an owner's estate. Where no designation is made, or where a designation has been made but is revoked and no designation has been made, the voting owner of each condo shall be the group composed of all its owners; any or all of such owners may be present at any meeting of the voting owners and, if those present act unanimously, may vote or take any other action as a voting owner, either in person or by proxy.

D) If a person, partnership or corporation owns more than one condo, he or it shall have the votes for each condo owned. In the event the record owner or owners have pledged their vote regarding special matters to another, only the vote of the pledgee will be recognized in regards to the special matters upon, which the vote is so pledged; provided that written notice of such pledge shall have been given to the Board prior to the vote. Amendments to this Section shall only be effective upon the written consent of all of the voting owners and the respective Security Holders, if any.

Section Eight
Use of Property and Condo

A) The building and the residence condo are intended for and restricted to the use by a single family as a residence and for no other purpose, excepting that within the building there may be carried on the normal management functions of the Association.

B) Garage apartments are intended for and restricted to use for storage of vehicles.

C) There shall be no obstruction of the common areas and nothing shall be stored therein except as may be expressly permitted by rules adopted by that Association and/or its Board of Directors, hereinafter called "Board".

D) The limited common areas and facilities are for the sole and exclusive use of the residence condo for which they are reserved.

E) The Association, acting through its Board, shall have power to impose reasonable rules for the use and occupancy of any of the property and to amend the same from time to time and all condo owners or occupants shall comply with the building rules from time to time in effect. The guiding rules shall be a part of the Bylaws.

Section Nine
Service or Process

John Q. Devloper, whose place of business is 999 Soaring Hill Road, Columbia, MD 21045, is hereby designated as the initial person to receive service of process in the causes provided in the Act.

Section Ten
Insurance

A) The Board shall purchase and carry at all times insurance, by insurance carriers rated to be "AAA" or better by Best's Insurance Reports, and licensed to do business in the State of Maryland, for indemnification of loss of real property whether owned independently or in common for the benefit of the Association and owners. Coverage shall be for the full replacement value of the common areas and the condos without discount for accrued depreciation, payable as the owners and their Security Holders, if any, as their interests may appear, which policy or policies shall provide for separate protection for each condo to the full insurable replacement value thereof without discount for accrued depreciation and a separate loss payable endorsement in favor of the Security Holder of each condo, if any.

B) The Board shall purchase and carry at all times liability insurance with respect to the Property and all operations, which coverage shall insure against any and all claims, damages or liability on account of injury to persons, including death and damage to, or the destruction of the property of others. Such liability insurance shall insure the Association and each owner, except for personal property and the personal liability of the owners arising from any and all personal activities. The minimum limits to be maintained shall be the Bodily Injury Liability $500,000.00 and the Property Damage Liability $100,000.00.

C) The Board shall purchase and carry at all times the necessary Employer's Liability and Workman's Compensation insurance for the protection of the Association and owners.

D) The Board, or its nominee, shall act as the insurance trustee for the benefit of the Association, owners and holders of security interests.

E) Security instruments between individual condo owners and the lenders may provide for such lenders to apply proceeds from insurance to the secured indebtedness, in which case the trustee shall disburse the insurance proceeds as directed by such lenders. To the extent that the insurance proceeds are not so applied the trustee shall disburse any proceeds as follows:

1. Payment of the cost of rebuilding, repairing or restoration if any, and

2. If the damaged area is not to be rebuilt, repaired or restored or if any insurance proceeds remain after such action, such proceeds shall be disbursed as follows:

   a. To Security Holders if any, as their interest may appear, and

   b. The balance of such proceeds to the owners in proportion to the loss incurred by each.

Section Eleven
Damage or Destruction of the Building and/or Site

A) If a building is damaged by fire or other insured casualty and the damaged is limited to a single condo, all insurance proceeds shall be paid to the Association, unless otherwise provided in the security instrument, for the benefit of the owner and the Security Holder to the extent necessary to rebuild, repair or restore such condo in accordance with the original plans and specifications as filed. The balance, if any, shall be paid to the owner or the Security Holder as their interest may appear.

B) If such damage extends to two or more condo units, or extends to any part of the common area, the Board shall collect the insurance proceeds as provided herein and obtain firm bids (including an obligation to supply a performance bond) from two or more responsible contractors to rebuild, repair or restore the damaged areas in accordance with the original plans and specifications of the building as filed, modified as may be necessary to comply with the then applicable Governmental rules and regulations and shall, as soon as possible thereafter, call a special meeting of the owners to consider such bids. Such special meeting shall be called by written notice given to each owner at least ten days prior to the date set for such meeting. If the Board fails to do so within 60 days after the casualty occurs, any owner may obtain such bids, and call and conduct such meeting after the same notice. At such meeting, the owners may, by two-thirds vote of the total percentage of ownership, elect to reject all such bids and not to rebuild, repair or restore the Property. Failure to thus reject all such bids shall authorize the Board to accept the bid it considers most favorable.

C) Failure to call a special meeting for the purpose of repairing, rebuilding or restoring the Property within 90 days from the date that the damage occurred shall be deemed for all purposes a decision not to rebuild, repair or restore the Property, provided however, that the prior written approval of the Security Holder upon each apartment must be obtained in order to sell the Property in lieu of rebuilding, repairing or restoring the same.

Section Twelve
Procedures for Combining or Subdividing

A) The Developer may combine or sub-divide any one or more condos or any parts thereof which he owns and may allocate the value of the combined or subdivided condos to the ultimate portions so established in any manner he deems desirable and may file amendments to this declaration executed and acknowledged by him setting forth such combinations or subdivisions and the allocation of value.

B) A resolution adopted by condo owners, excepting as herein before provided for the Developer having 60 percent of the votes, may provide for the combination or sub-division or both of any apartment or apartments or of the common limited common areas and facilities or any parts thereof, and the means for accomplishing such combination of sub-division or both and may also provide in conjunction there with for the appropriate amendments to this declaration, the Bylaws, or to any other document or agreements affected thereby. Prior to any such combining or sub-dividing, the written approval for such action by the Security Holder, if any, shall be presented to the Board.

C) In the event of any combining or sub-dividing under either of the above provisions, the space combined or sub-divided shall have, after such combination or sub-division the same percentage of total value that the space involved had prior to such combination or sub-division.

Section Thirteen
Bylaws

Bylaws for the administration of the Association, the Property and for other purposes not inconsistent with the Act, shall be adopted by the Association by a 60 percent vote of membership at a meeting to be held for that purpose. Notice of the time, place and purpose of such meeting shall be delivered to each condo owner at least three days prior to such meeting. Amendments to the Bylaws may be adopted by the same vote at a meeting similarly called. Administration of the Property shall be by a Board of five or more directors elected from among the condo owners.

Section Fourteen
Guarantees

The Developer's responsibility to the condo owners shall be limited to defects in the construction of the building or in the installation or operation of any mechanical equipment therein due to improper workmanship or materials or as a result of work or materials at variance with what was specified. Such defects will be promptly corrected at his own cost and expense; provided that he is given written notice of the existence of such defects within one year from the date that the City of Easton issues an occupancy permit for the particular building. He further agrees to assign to the Association all guarantees from subcontractors or suppliers of materials running in favor of the Developer to the extent that such guarantees are assignable.

Section Fifteen
Retention of Ownership and Use

The Developer has the right to retain an ownership interest in condo units. In addition thereto he and/or his agents may use the said condo and necessary common areas for sale and promotional purposes.

Section Sixteen
Entry for Repairs

The Board or its agents may enter any condo or any limited common areas and facilities when necessary in connection with any maintenance or construction activity. Such entry shall be made with a minimum of inconvenience to the condo owner and any damaged caused by such entry shall be repaired by the Board or its agents at its expense.

Section Seventeen
Monthly Assessments

A) All condo owners are obligated to pay monthly assessments imposed by the Association to meet all common expenses of the Property which may include premiums or insurance policies, as herein before more specifically set forth in Section IX. The assessment shall be made prorate according to the percent of undivided interest in the common areas and facilities owned by each condo owner. Such assessments may include monthly payments to a general operating reserve and a reserve fund for replacements for which provision may be made in the Bylaws. Assessments shall be payable in advance on the 1st day of each month, and shall bear interest at the rate of 1 percent per month, if not paid on or before the 10th day of the month for which the same are due. Any unpaid assessments shall constitute a lien upon the condo for which it is due. Such lien shall run in favor of the Association, and may be foreclosed by it through legal action instituted by its president as authorized by the Association's Board.

B) No condo owner may waive or otherwise escape liability for the assessments provided for herein by non-use of the common areas or abandonment of his apartment.

C) The Board shall utilize funds from the assessments herein to maintain the common areas in good repair and condition and will not permit waste.

D) Notice shall be given by the Board to the Security Holder of any condo unit of any delinquency in the payment of assessments which is more than 45 days overdue.

E) Nothing herein shall be construed as to make the assessment payments applicable to any Security Holder. In the event of a foreclosure or deed of trust sale, the new owner shall take the condo unit and related areas subject to and be responsible for the accrued assessments and interest thereon which shall be payable at the time of closing.

Section Eighteen
Collection of Assessments

A) A condo owner may be required, in accordance with the Bylaws of the Association, from time to time, to make a security deposit not in excess of 3 months' estimated monthly assessments, which may be collected as are other assessments. Such deposit shall be held in a separate fund, credited to such owner, and resort may be had thereto at any time when such owner is 10 days or more delinquent in paying his monthly or other assessments.

B) In any action to foreclose a lien on any condo for nonpayment of delinquent assessments, any judgment in favor of the Association rendered therein shall include a reasonable sum for attorney's fees and all costs and expenses reasonably incurred in preparation for or in the prosecution of said action, in addition to taxable costs permitted by law. From the time of commencement of any action to foreclose a lien against a condo for nonpayment of delinquent assessments, the owner of such condo shall pay to the Association the reasonable rental value of said condo to be fixed by the Board, and the plaintiff of any such foreclosure shall be entitled to the appointment of a receiver to collect the same. Provided: however, the right to collect rents as herein stated shall be subject to any assignment of rents and profits made to a Security Holder.

C) In addition to and not by way of limitation upon other methods of collection of any assessments, the Board shall have the right, after having given 10 days notice to any condo owner who is delinquent in paying his assessments, to cut off any or all utility services to the delinquent owner's apartment until such assessments are paid.

Section Nineteen
Structural Modifications

No structural modification or alterations in any apartment shall be made without specific prior authorization in writing from the Board and the prior written approval of all Security Holders of the property.

Section Twenty
Restriction on Conveyance of Apartments

A) In the event of any offer of, or sale, rental lease or conveyance of a condo, after the first conveyance thereof by the Developer, the Association or its designee shall have a right of first refusal to purchase, rent, or lease the same on the same conditions and at the same price and terms as are offered by the condo owner to any third person. Any attempt after the first conveyance to sell, rent, lease or convey any condo, without prior offer to the Association, shall be wholly null and void and shall confer no title, interest or right whatsoever upon the intended purchaser, tenant, lessee or grantee.

B) Should any condo owner desire to sell, rent, lease or convey a condo or any portion thereof, he shall, before making or accepting any offer, therefore, and before making any conveyance of the condo, give to each member of the Board written notice of his intent to sell, rent, lease or convey such condo, or any interest therein, which notice shall contain the terms of the offer he has received or which he wishes to accept or the terms of an acceptable offer he is prepared to make, and the name and address of the prospective purchaser, tenant or grantee. The giving of such notice to each member of the Board shall be proved by

58 Condominiums

filing with the Board proof of such notice consisting of an affidavit of service, acknowledgment of receipt of notice, or a signed certified mail return receipt.

C) The Board shall, within 10 days after the last of the members thereof has received such notice, either consent to the transaction specified in said notice, or by dated written notice to such owner designate one or more persons who are then condo owners, or any other person of reasonably satisfactory credit, who is willing, within 15 days for such designation, to purchase, lease, rent or accept the same terms and conditions are those specified in such owner's notice. Such owner may, within said 15 day period, either accept such new offer, if made, or withdraw or reject the offer specified in his notice to the Board, as well as such new offer, but he may not reject such new offer, if made, and continue to propose or accept the offer specified in his original notice. Failure of the Board to designate such person within said 10 day period, or failure of such person to make such an offer within the said 15 day period, shall be deemed consent by the Association to the transaction specified in said owner's notice, and he shall be free thereafter to make or accept the offer specified in his original notice, and to sell, lease, rent or convey said condo or interest therein to the prospective purchaser, tenant or grantee named, within 90 days after his original notice was given, but after the 90 days his right to proceed without compliance with the provisions herein shall cease.

D) The sub-leasing or sub-renting or assigning of a condo or any part thereof shall be subject to the same limitations and restrictions as are herein made applicable to the leasing or rental of any apartment, and the same procedures and other provisions of this Paragraph shall apply thereto.

E) In no event may garage apartments be sold to anyone who is not an owner or contract purchaser of a residence condo.

F) No condo owner shall have any right to sell, lease, sub-lease, rent, or convey his condo or any interest therein, except as expressly provided herein. The provisions, limitations and restrictions of this Paragraph shall not be waived by the Association notwithstanding the fact that any condo owner may have previously leased, sub-leased, rented, conveyed, sold or assigned his apartment or any interest therein in conformity with the provisions hereof or otherwise.

G) The restrictions on sale, conveyance, leasing or rental of any condo contained in this Section Twenty except as stated in sub-section E hereof, shall not apply to the Developer.

H) The restrictions on sale, conveyance, leasing or rental of any condo contained in this Section Twenty, except as stated in sub-section E hereof, shall not apply to any financial institution which has by foreclosure or other process of realization upon security become owner of possessor of any condo. This proviso shall not, however, exempt any purchaser from or tenant of any such institution from the provisions of this section.

Section Twenty-One
Certificates of Compliance

An officer of the Association shall be empowered under rules established by the Bylaws to provide certificates in acknowledged, recorded form showing whether or not any right of first refusal has been complied with and whether or not any assessments due the Association have been paid.

Section Twenty-Two
Amendment to the Declaration

A) This Declaration may be amended, consistent with the Laws of the State of Maryland and pertaining thereto, upon the giving of written notice of a meeting to all condo owners and Security Holders, if any, setting forth the proposed amendment by certified mail, return receipt requested, to each such owner and Security Holder at the last known address, not less than 10 days prior to the meeting, which meeting shall be held upon the Property or at such other place within Talbot County, Maryland, as may be specified in the notice of the meeting. For any such amendment to become effective, a resolution to amend the Declaration must be approved by the affirmative vote of not less than 60 percent of the percentage votes of the owners as established in Section Seven and all Security Holders.

B) Nothing herein shall be construed as to authorize an amendment which discriminates against any apartment owner, nor against any apartment or class or group of apartments unless the apartment owners so affected shall consent.

C) No amendment shall be effective for any purpose unless set forth in a properly prepared "Amendment of Declaration" which shall refer to this Declaration and be recorded in the office of the Auditor of Talbot County, Maryland.

Section Twenty-Three
Reservation of Rights

Apex Mortgage Corporation has financed the construction of the buildings and improvement on the Site and holds a note and deeds of trust on the Property in the approximate amount of $300,000.00 which deeds of trust and modifications thereto are recorded under Auditor's receiving No. 71122000068, No. 7204110059, No. 7207240110 and No. 7207200569. Apex Mortgage Corporation waives no rights and consents to no modifications of its rights herein and retains all security interests against the Property, which shall include the condo buildings, the common areas and facilities, the Site and the improvements thereon, except insofar as the rights of the Apex Mortgage Corporation may be specifically relinquished by partial release of the said deed of trust for residential condo, garage apartments, and percentage of common areas.

Section Twenty-Four
Condemnation

Should the Property or any part or appurtenance thereof or right or interest therein be taken or damaged by reason of anybody having the power of eminent domain, all compensation and damages for or on account of the Property shall be payable to the Board as trustee for all condo owners and Security Holders, of any, according to the loss or damage of their respective interest in their condos and common areas

Where applicable, nothing herein shall be construed to limit or abrogate the rights of any deed of trust beneficiary of any condo unit as set forth in Paragraph 14, Master Form of Deed of Trust as recorded on June 12, 1985 within the Talbot County Auditor's office under Receiving No. 6188051 and is found in Volume 5428 of Mortgages, Page 26 and any amendment thereto which is duly recorded which are by this reference made a part thereof.

Section Twenty-Five
Miscellaneous

Unless some other meaning and intent are apparent from the context, the singular shall include the plural and vice versa and masculine, feminine and neuter words shall be used interchangeably.

Section Twenty-Six
File Number of Floor Plans

The floor plans of the building referred to herein were filed with the Auditor of Talbot County, Maryland, simultaneously with the recording of this Declaration under Auditor's file No. _____, in Volume _____ of Condominiums, pages _____ through _____.

Executed this 25th day of August 1985, at Easton, Maryland.

_____
John Q. Developer

STATE OF MARYLAND
COUNTY OF TALBOT

On this 25th day of August 1985, before me, the undersigned, a notary public in and for the State of Maryland, duly commissioned and sworn, personally appeared John Q. Developer, to me known to be the individual described in and who executed the foregoing document, and acknowledged to me that he signed and sealed the same as his free and voluntary act and deed for the uses and purposes therein stated.

WITNESS MY HAND and official seal affixed hereto the day and year first hereinabove written

_____
NOTARY PUBLIC in and for the State of Maryland, residing in Easton

Appendix B
By-Laws

BY-LAWS OF
ASSOCIATION OF APARTMENT OWNERS
OF CAMELOT COURT

ARTICLE I
Principal Office

The principle office of the Association shall be located at 1234 Canterbury Lane, Easton, Maryland.

The Association may maintain such other offices as may be necessary for the business of the Association.

ARTICLE II
Membership

Section 1. *Eligibility*. The fee owners of the condos of Camelot Court will constitute the Association of condo Owners (herein referred to as "Association"). Corporations, partnerships, associations and other legal entities, trustees under and express trust and other fiduciaries, as well as natural persons, shall be eligible for membership if otherwise qualified. Provided that mortgages and deed of trust beneficiaries shall be considered "fee owners" for the purposes herein once a lawsuit has been commenced to realize on their security and a copy of the summons and complaint has been received by the Secretary of the Board.

Section 2. *Joint Membership.* Persons owning a condo as joint tenants, tenants in common, community property, or other fee ownership involving more than one owner, shall be joint members of the Association, but the sum total of their vote shall not exceed the percentage of interest for voting power assigned to their condo in the recorded Declaration, or any lawful amendment thereto.

Section 3. *Persons Under Disability.* Minors and persons declared legally incompetent shall be eligible for membership in the Association, if otherwise qualified, but shall not be permitted to vote except through a legally appointed, qualified and acting guardian of their estate voting in their behalf.

Section 4. *Register of Members.* Members of the Association who sell or convey their interest in condos shall promptly report such fact to the Board of Directors (hereinafter referred to as "Board") and furnish the Board with the name and address of their successors in interest. The Board shall cause a register to be kept, containing the names and addresses of all members of the Association. Persons who become eligible for membership in the Association shall furnish the Board with a copy of any document under which they assert ownership to a condo, or any interest therein, at least twenty-four hours prior to the time of any meeting of the Association at which they desire to vote, and in default thereof, voting power for the condo involved shall remain in the person who, according to the records of the Association, is entitled to cast such vote.

ARTICLE III
Meetings to Members

Section 1. *Place.* Meetings of the members of the Association shall be held at the principal office of the Association, or at such other suitable place in the City of Easton, Maryland, as may be convenient to the membership and may be designated from time to time by the Board.

Section 2. *Annual Meeting.* The first annual meeting of the Association shall be held at such time and on such date as may be contained in a written notice given to each member by John Q. Builder no less than twenty days prior to said meeting. Thereinafter, the annual meeting of the Association shall be held at the same time and on the same day in the succeeding year and every year thereafter. If such day is a legal holiday, then the annual meeting shall be held on the next business day following. At such annual meeting the members shall elect by ballot a Board in accordance with the provisions of the Declaration of Condominium and these Bylaws and there shall be transacted such other business as may properly come before the meeting.

Section 3. *Special Meetings.* It shall be the duty of the President to call a special meeting of the Association as directed by resolution of the Board, or upon the written request of not less than one-third of the members of the Association. A meeting called at the request of the members shall be held at such time as the President may fix, which time shall not be less than ten or more than thirty days after receipt of the written request.

Section 4. *Notice of Meetings.* It shall be the duty of the Secretary to mail a notice of each annual and special meeting stating the business that will be placed before such meeting as well as the time and place where it is to be held, at least ten but not more than twenty days prior to such meeting to each member or his proxy registered as herein provided or to deliver the same to him or some other person of suitable age and discretion at the address of the condo in which he holds the ownership or at such other address as such member shall have furnished to the Secretary in writing. At least ten but not more than twenty days written notice shall be given as provided herein to each member and to all mortgagees and deed of trust beneficiaries as to any meeting at which there will be submitted to a vote of the members, an amendment to the Declaration or to these Bylaws and a copy of the members of the Association may be waived in writing at any time or by his appearance thereat, excepting when a members appears specially to challenge the propriety of the meeting due to the lack of proper notice.

Section 5. *Quorum.* Except as may be otherwise provided herein or in the recorded Declaration, the presence in person or by proxy of members of the Association holding fifty-one percent of the voting power of all condo owners, shall constitute a quorum for the transaction of business at any meeting of members of the Association.

Section 6. *Adjourned Meetings.* If any meeting of the members cannot be organized because a quorum is not in attendance, either in person or by proxy, the members present may adjourn the meeting to a time not less than forty-eight hours and not more than ninety-six hours from the time the original meeting was called and those who attend such an adjourned meeting, although less than a majority of the membership, shall nevertheless constitute a quorum for the purpose or purposes of said meeting, provided at least twenty-five percent of the voting power of all condos is present, either in person or by proxy and provided further that no amendment to the recorded Declaration or to these Bylaws may be adopted except as provided for herein.

Section 7. *Voting.* If a husband and wife who are joint members by virtue of ownership of a condo or interest therein as community property are in attendance at a meeting, their vote shall be cast by the husband unless he has appointed his wife as his proxy as herein provided. If a husband and wife who are joint members because of such community ownership are not both present at the meeting, their vote may be cast by the spouse who is present. The vote of all other joint members shall be split and each as such joint members shall be entitled to vote a fractional portion of the voting power assigned to his condo equal to his percentage of ownership there, unless otherwise provided for by proxy in accordance with these Bylaws.

Section 8. *Majority Vote.* Except as otherwise provided by law, by the recorded Declaration or these Bylaws, all questions submitted to vote at a meeting or adjourned meeting duly called, where a quorum, as defined by these Bylaws, is in attendance shall require for passage or adoption the affirmative vote of sixty percent of the voting power represented by the members in attendance in person or by proxy.

Section 9. *Proxies.* The authority given by any condo owner to another person to represent him at meetings of the Association shall be in writing, signed by such owner and filed with the Secretary, and unless limited by its items shall continue until revoked by writing filed with the Secretary or by the death or incapacity of such owner. Voting rights transferred or pledged by mortgage, deed of trust or agreement sale of any condo or interest therein, a true copy of which is filed with Board through the Secretary, shall be exercised only by the person designated in such instrument until the written release or other termination thereof is filed with the Board in like manner.

Section 10. *Order of Business.* The order of business at meetings of the Association shall be done as follows:

    a. Roll Call
    b. Proof of Notice of Meeting or Waiver Notice.
    c. Reading of Minutes of Preceding Meeting
    d. Reports of Officers
    e. Reports of Committees
    f. Election of Directors (Annual Meeting or Special Meeting called for such purpose)
    g. Unfinished Business
    h. New Business

ARTICLE IV
Board of Directors

Section 1. *Number and Qualifications.* The affairs of the Association shall be governed by a Board of Directors composed of seven persons who shall be elected by and from the members of the Association. If a corporation is a member of the Association, any one or more of its officers, directors or stockholders may be elected to the Board, as well as any one or more members of a partnership which is a member.

Section 2. *Powers and Duties.* The Board shall have the powers and duties necessary for the administration of the affairs of the Association and may do all such acts and things as are not by law or these Bylaws directed to be exercised and done by the owners.

Section 3. *Other Duties.* In addition to duties imposed by these Bylaws, or by resolutions of the Association, the Board shall be responsible for the following:

a. Care, maintenance and surveillance of the Property, which shall include the condominium building and the Site and the improvements thereon;

b. Collection of monthly and other assessments from the owners;

c. Designation and dismissal of the personnel necessary for the maintenance and operation of the property, the common areas and facilities.

Section 4. *Agent.* The Board may employ for the Association a management agent at a compensation established by the Board, to perform such duties and services as the Board shall authorize, including but not limited to the duties listed in Section 3 of this Article.

Section 5. *Election and Term of Office.* At the first annual meeting of the Association, a Board of Directors shall be elected, the term of office of two directors shall be fixed for three years, the term of office for three other directors shall be fixed at two years and the term of office for the remaining two directors shall be fixed at one year. At the expiration of the initial term of office of each such director, his successor shall be elected to serve a term of three years; the directors shall hold office until their successors have been elected.

Section 6. *Vacancies.* Vacancies in the Board caused by reason other than the removal of a director by a vote of the Association, shall be filled by a vote of the majority of the remaining directors, even though they may constitute less than a quorum, and each person so elected shall be a director for the balance of the term of the director whose vacancy he filled.

Section 7. *Removal of Directors.* At any annual or special meeting of the Association duly called, any one or more of the directors may be removed, with or without cause, by the affirmative vote of fifty-one percent of the voting power of all condo owners and a successor may then and there be elected to fill the vacancy. Any director whose removal has been proposed by the owners shall be given an opportunity to be heard at the meeting.

Section 8. *Compensation.* No compensation shall be paid to directors for their services.

Section 9. *Organization Meeting.* The first meeting of the newly elected Board shall be held within ten days of their election at such place as shall be fixed by the directors at the meeting at which the directors were elected, provided a majority of the whole Board was present at said meeting.

Section 10. *Regular Meetings.* Regular meetings by the Board may be held at such time, date and place as shall be determined by the directors at the organization meeting. The directors shall set the time, date and place for two regular meetings of the Board to be held during the coming year. Reminder notices of such regular meetings of the Board shall be given to each director personally, by mail, telephone or telegraph at least ten days prior to the day fixed for such meeting.

Section 11. *Special Meetings.* Special meetings of the Board may be called by the President on three days prior notice to each director given personally, by mail, telephone or telegraph. The notice shall state the time, place and purpose of the meeting. Special meetings of the Board of Directors shall be called by the President or Secretary in like manner and on like notice on the written request of at least three directors within ten days after receipt of such request.

Section 12. *Waiver of Notice.* Before or after any meeting of the Board, any director may in writing waive notice of such meeting and such waiver shall be deemed equivalent to the serving of such notice. Attendance by a director at any meeting of the board shall be a waiver of notice by him of the time and place thereof. If all the directors are present at any meeting of the Board, no notice shall be required and any business may be transacted at such meeting.

Section 13. *Quorum.* At all meetings of the Board, a majority of all the directors shall constitute a quorum for the transaction of business, and the acts of the majority of the directors present at a meeting at which a quorum is present shall be the acts of the Board.

Section 14. *Fidelity Bonds.* The Board shall require that all officers and employees of the Association handling or responsible for funds of the Association furnish adequate fidelity bonds. The premiums on such bonds shall be paid by the Association as a common expense.

ARTICLE V
Officers

Section 1. *Designation.* The principal officers of the Association shall be a President, a Vice-President, a Secretary and a Treasurer all of whom shall be elected by and from the Board. Any two of the offices of Vice-President, Secretary or Treasurer may be combined into one person. The directors may appoint an Assistant

Treasurer and an Assistant Secretary and such other officers as may be necessary in their judgement.

Section 2. *Election of Officers.* The officers of the Association shall be elected annually by the Board at the organization meeting of each new Board.

Section 3. *Removal of Officers.* At any annual or special meeting of the Association duly called, any one or more of the officers may be removed, with or without cause and a successor elected to fill the vacancy at any regular meeting of the Board or any special meeting of the Board called for that purpose.

Section 4. *President.* The President shall be the chief executive office of the Association. He shall preside at all meetings of the Association and of the Board and shall have all powers and duties usually vested in the office of the President.

Section 5. *Vice-President.* The Vice-President shall perform the duties of the President when the President is absent or unable to act and shall perform such other duties as may be prescribed by the Board.

Section 6. *Secretary.* The Secretary shall keep the minutes of all meetings of the Board and of the Association. He or she shall, in addition, perform all duties incident to the office of Secretary of a business corporation.

Section 7. *Treasurer.* The Treasurer shall have responsibility for corporate funds and securities and shall be responsible for keeping full and accurate accounts of all receipts and disbursements in books belonging to the Association.

Section 8. *Other Officers.* Other officers of the Association shall have such authority and shall perform such duties as the Board may prescribe. An assistant secretary or treasurer shall also have all powers of the Secretary and/or Treasurer in the absence of such officers.

ARTICLE VI
Committees

Section 1. *Committees of Directors.* The Board may designate one or more committees of directors, each of which shall consist of two or more directors. Such committees, to the extent provided in the resolution establishing the committee, shall have and exercise the authority of the Board in the management of the Association, but the designation of such committee shall not operate to relieve the Board of any responsibility imposed upon it.

Section 2. *Other Committees.* Other committees, not having or exercising the authority of the Board in the management of the Association, may be designated by the President or a majority of directors.

ARTICLE VII
Indemnification

The Association shall indemnify and hold harmless each person who shall serve at any time as a director of the Association, or as an officer without compensation, from any and all claims and liabilities to which such person shall become subject, by reason of his having served as a director or uncompensated officer of the Association or by reason or any action alleged to have been taken or omitted to be taken by such person. The Association shall reimburse each such person for all legal and other expenses reasonably incurred by him in connection with any such claim or liability, provided, however, that no such person shall be indemnified against or be reimbursed for any expense incurred with any claim or liability arising out of his own fraud, bad faith or willful misconduct.

ARTICLE IX
Miscellaneous

Unless some other meaning and intent are apparent from the context, the singular shall include the plural and vice versa. Masculine, feminine and neuter words shall be used interchangeably.

Appendix C
Condominium Rules

CAMELOT COURT
CONDOMINIUM RULES

IN CASE OF FIRE
1. Dial 911 to notify the Fire Department.
2. Activate the Fire Alarm Box on your floor. When activated, this serves as a warning to residents.
3. Do not use elevators as an exit route, use the stairs.

COMMON AREAS
Hallways, elevators, pool area, and recreation areas should be cared for as relates to cleanliness, damage, and/or abuse as if these belonged to us individually. We ask that particular care is taken with all grocery carts, moving of furniture, etc., so as not to cause damage. Movers shall be so directed.

Additional furnishings (e.g. furniture, wall hangings, plants, etc.) that residents desire to place on individual floors (in accordance with fire safety regulations) shall first have the consent of all residents on that particular floor, then be submitted to the Board of Directors for final approval. In short, *nothing* shall be placed in any of the common areas without the prior approval of floor residents and/or the Board of Directors.

Children are not permitted to play in common areas such as the sauna, lobbies, garages, stairways, hallways, elevators and bicycle room.

GENERAL

Noise Levels

This is of great concern to all of us. The hour of operation of all appliances should be planned so that such operation does not disturb your neighbor. Discretion is encouraged. On the topic of noise levels generated by radios, stereos, televisions, parties, etc., remember our good neighbor policy.

Fireplaces

Fireplaces are not to be used for heating purposes. They are for your enjoyment on a controlled basis. Again, discretion should be used.

Exterior Appearance of Buildings

It is intended that the exterior of the building present a uniform appearance at all times. Any request for a deviation must be referred to the Board of Directors.

Sale, Rent or Lease of Unit

In the case of a sale, rent or lease of a unit, please refer to Declaration Section XX for protocol. Reminder: owners are responsible to pay an administration fee of $50.00 each time a unit is vacated by reason of rent or sale.

DECKS

All activities on decks must be disturbance free. Decks should be kept clean and the railing should be kept clear. Decks are not to be used for charcoal broiling. Articles and debris are not to be thrown from decks.

PARKING STALLS

Stalls shall be kept free of oil and grease. Please remember the guest parking area is head-in parking only.

PETS

1. Pets shall always be on a leash.
2. Only small dogs, cats and birds are permitted.
3. Residents are responsible for the prevention of unsanitary conditions, odors, and noise caused by a pet.
4. No pet is permitted in the fenced-in backyard.
5. Only pets belonging to residents of Camelot Court will be permitted on the property.

RECREATION ROOM

The Recreation Room is used for:

1. The Board of Directors' and Owners' meetings.
2. Residents' parties (by reservation).
3. Other activities as approved by the Board.

The room must be reserved in advance (if possible, one week) for group use. The noise level must be controlled and cleanup must follow the closing of the function for which the room was reserved. It is the responsibility of the hosting resident to restore the facilities to the original degree of cleanliness. This includes hallways, elevators, lobbies, and parking areas. Reservations may be made by calling our custodian. Children under the age of 18 must have responsible and adequate adult supervision at all times.

SAUNA FACILITIES

These facilities are for the use of residents and their adult guests. Any adult using the sauna does so at her/his own risk. Cleanup after use will be the responsibility of the resident.

SECURITY

Care should always be taken to keep exterior doors secured at all times. Garage doors should be used for household moving. Reproduction of keys require Board approval. Doors should never, *repeat never*, be opened to strangers. Instead, visitors should be directed to ring the unit of whomever they have come to visit.

Although the above rules are officially cited as CAMELOT COURT CONDOMINIUM RULES, we should look upon them as an example of a "GOOD NEIGHBOR POLICY practice." Together we can make this condominium living a pleasant ongoing experience for all of us.

POOL RULES FOR CAMELOT COURT OWNERS' ASSOCIATION:

1. Residents shall be answerable for their guests' conduct and responsible for damage and/or liability.
2. Residents and their guest(s) shall observe the pool rules as posted. All persons using the pool do so at their own risk.
3. Bathers shall remove all suntan lotions, ointments, pins, and curlers before entering the pool area and should be reasonably dry before entering the building.

4. Use of the pool and pool area is between 8:00 a.m. and 10:00 p.m.
5. Children under the age of 18 years of age are to have responsible and adequate adult supervision at all times.
6. No pets are allowed in the pool area or in the fenced-in lawn area on the west side of the building.
7. Glass, ceramics, china or other breakables are not permitted in the pool area.
8. Charcoal cooking is permitted in the pool area provided safety precautions are followed and proper cleanup is assured.
9. No running, pushing, boisterous or loud conduct, high volume playing of radios or musical instruments is permitted in the pool area.
10. Reservations for use of the pool and/or recreation room can be made by calling the custodian. No exclusive use of the pool will be granted. Residents and their adult guests may use the sauna room facilities. Children are not permitted to use the sauna room. As good neighbors, please take care to leave these facilities in the same condition as you found them. When a reservation is made and approved, it shall be posted in the elevators at least 48 hours prior to the reservation date so that others can plan their activities accordingly. When calling the custodian for a reservation, the following information should be supplied — please see next page:

RESERVATION FOR THE USE OF POOL/RECREATION ROOM

☐ Pool   ☐ Recreation Room

Date: _____

Time From: _____ To: _____

Number of Guests (must be more than 8):
_____

Resident's Name:
_____

Telephone: _____

Request for chairs (number):
_____

Exhibit A: Unit Number and Location

Residence Number	Location	Approximate Area	Number of Rooms
N-101	NW portion of first floor of north building	1,380 square feet	5 plus 2 bathrooms
N-102	NE portion of first floor of north building	1,220 square feet	5 plus 2 bathrooms
N-103	N center portion of first and second floors of north building	1,570 square feet	6 plus 1 ½ bathrooms
N-104	S center portion of first and second floors of north building	1,570 square feet	6 plus 1 ½ bathrooms
N-105	SE portion of first floor	950 square	4 plus 1
N-106	SW portion of first floor	1,050	4 plus 1
N-201	NW portion of second	1,380	5 plus 2
N-202	NE portion of second	1,220	5 plus 2
N-203	SE portion of second	1,220	5 plus 2
N-204	SW center portion of second floor of north building	1,380 square feet	5 plus 2 bathrooms
N-205	SE center portion of second floor of north	1,380 square feet	5 plus 2 bathrooms

86 Condominiums

Residence Number	Location	Approximate Area	Number of Rooms
N-206	SW portion of second floor of north building	1,380 square feet	5 plus 2 bathrooms
N-301	NW portion of third floor of north building	1,380 square feet	5 plus 2 bathrooms
N-302	NE portion of third floor of north building	1,220 square feet	5 plus 2 bathrooms
N-303	N center portion of third and fourth floors of north building	1,570 square feet	6 plus 1 ½ bathrooms
N-304	S center portion of third and fourth floors of north building	1,570 square feet	6 plus 1 ½ bathrooms
N-305	SE portion of third floor of north building	1,220 square feet	5 plus 2 bathrooms
N-306	SW portion of third floor of north building	1,380 square feet	5 plus 2 bathrooms
N-401	NW portion of fourth floor of north building	1,380 square feet	5 plus 2 bathrooms
N-402	NE portion of fourth floor of north building	1,220 square feet	5 plus 2 bathrooms
S-101	SW portion of first floor of south building	1,380 square feet	5 plus 2 bathrooms
S-102	SE portion of first floor of south building	1,220 square feet	5 plus 2 bathrooms
S-103	S center portion of first and second floors of south building	1,570 square feet	6 plus 1 ½ bathrooms

Residence Number	Location	Approximate Area	Number of Rooms
S-104	N center portion of first and second floors of	1,570 square feet	6 plus 1 ½ bathrooms
S-105	NE portion of first floor of south building	950 square feet	4 plus 1 bathroom
S-106	NW portion of first floor of south building	1,050 square feet	4 plus 1 bathroom
S-201	SW portion of second floor of south building	1,380 square feet	5 plus 2 bathrooms
S-202	SE portion of second floor of south building	1,220 square feet	5 plus 2 bathrooms
S-203	NE portion of second floor of south building	1,220 square feet	5 plus 2 bathrooms
S-204	SE portion of second floor of south building	1,220 square feet	5 plus 2 bathrooms
S-205	SW center portion of second floor of south building	1,380 square feet	5 plus 2 bathrooms
S-206	NW portion of second floor of south building	1,380 square feet	5 plus 2 bathrooms
S-301	SW portion of third floor of south building	1,380 square feet	5 plus 2 bathrooms
S-302	SE portion of third floor of south building	1,220 square feet	5 plus 2 bathrooms
S-303	S center portion of third and fourth floors of south building	1,570 square feet	6 plus 1 ½ bathrooms

88 Condominiums

Residence Number	Location	Approximate Area	Number of Rooms
S-304	N center portion of third	1,570	6 plus 1 ½
S-305	NE portion of third floor	1,220	5 plus 2
S-306	NW portion of third floor of south building	1,380 square feet	5 plus 2 bathrooms
S-401	SW portion of fourth floor of south building	1,380 square feet	5 plus 2 bathrooms
S-402	SE portion of fourth floor of south building	1,220 square feet	5 plus 2 bathrooms

Access

Each residence has access to the common hall, stairways and elevator located in the west center of the floor of each building on which such apartment is situated, hence via such elevator or stairways to the lobby entrance to each building, and to the surface level of each building containing the garage apartments, and from that level to the public street.

Each residence has the exclusive right to use the lanai adjoining such residence, which lanai is listed herein as a limited common area; and each residence has the exclusive right to use of a storage locker on the surface level or first floor, bearing the same number as the condo.

Garage Areas

Garages 1 through and including 6 are located in the southwest section of the surface level of the south building and are numbered south to north. Garages 7 through and including 12 are located in the northwest section of the surface level of the south building and are numbered south to north. Garages 13 and 14 are located on the surface level between the south and north buildings and are numbered south to north. Garages 15 through and including 20 are located in the southwest section of the surface level of the north building and are numbered south to north. Garage apartments 21 through and including 26 are located in the NW section of the surface level of the north building and are numbered south to north. Garages 27 through and including 30 are located in the SE section of the surface level of the south building and are numbered south to north. Garages 31 through and including 34 are located in the NE section of the surface level of the south building and are number south to north. Garages 35 through and including 40 are located in the SE section of the surface level of the north building and are numbered south to north.

Exhibit B: Unit Value

Apt. Number	Value	% of Ownership
N-101	$135,000.00	2.314%
N-102	$135,000.00	2.314%
N-103	$145,000.00	2.486%
N-104	$145,000.00	2.486%
N-105	$125,000.00	2.14%
N-106	$120,000.00	2.06%
N-201	$140,000.00	2.40%
N-202	$140,000.00	2.40%
N-203	$140,000.00	2.40%
N-204	$135,000.00	2.314%
N-205	$145,000.00	2.486%
N-206	$140,000.00	2.40%
N-301	$148,000.00	2.537%
N-302	$145,000.00	2.486%
N-303	$150,000.00	2.571%
N-304	$150,000.00	2.571%
N-305	$145,000.00	2.486%
N-306	$148,000.00	2.537%
N-401	$148,000.00	2.537%
N-402	$145,000.00	2.486%

Apt. Number	Value	% of Ownership
S-101	$138,000.00	2.366%
S-102	$140,000.00	2.40%
S-103	$147,000.00	2.52%
S-104	$148,000.00	2.537%
S-105	$120,000.00	2.06%
S-106	$120,000.00	2.06%
S-201	$144,000.00	2.469%
S-202	$142,000.00	2.434%
S-203	$142,000.00	2.434%
S-204	$140,000.00	2.40%
S-205	$148,000.00	2.537%
S-206	$142,000.00	2.424%
S-301	$150,000.00	2.571%
S-302	$150,000.00	2.571%
S-303	$165,000.00	2.829%
S-304	$145,000.00	2.486%
S-305	$148,000.00	2.537%
S-306	$150,000.00	2.571%
S-401	$155,000.00	2.657%
S-402	$155,000.00	2.657%

Exhibit C: Garage Unit Value

Garage Number	Value	% of Ownership
1	$3,000.00	0.05143%
2	$3,000.00	0.05143%
3	$3,000.00	0.05143%
4	$3,000.00	0.05143%
5	$3,000.00	0.05143%
6	$3,000.00	0.05143%
7	$3,000.00	0.05143%
8	$3,000.00	0.05143%
9	$3,000.00	0.05143%
10	$3,000.00	0.05143%
11	$3,000.00	0.05143%
12	$3,000.00	0.05143%
13	$3,000.00	0.05143%
14	$3,000.00	0.05143%
15	$3,000.00	0.05143%
16	$3,000.00	0.05143%
17	$3,000.00	0.05143%
18	$3,000.00	0.05143%
19	$3,000.00	0.05143%
20	$3,000.00	0.05143%

Garage Number	Value	% of Ownership
21	$3,000.00	0.05143%
22	$3,000.00	0.05143%
23	$3,000.00	0.05143%
24	$3,000.00	0.05143%
25	$3,000.00	0.05143%
26	$3,000.00	0.05143%
27	$3,000.00	0.05143%
28	$3,000.00	0.05143%
29	$3,000.00	0.05143%
30	$3,000.00	0.05143%
31	$3,000.00	0.05143%
32	$3,000.00	0.05143%
33	$3,000.00	0.05143%
34	$3,000.00	0.05143%
35	$3,000.00	0.05143%
36	$3,000.00	0.05143%
37	$3,000.00	0.05143%
38	$3,000.00	0.05143%
39	$3,000.00	0.05143%
40	$3,000.00	0.05143%

About the Author

Frank J. La Mar has pursued a long-standing affair with real estate and has personally occupied, and owned for investment purposes, a dozen homes and condominiums on both the East and West coasts. With a formal education in business administration and as a licensed realtor, real estate has proven to be a sure and steady asset-enhancing pursuit for the author.

Mr. La Mar and his wife have four grown children, three loving grand-daughters and two adorable great-grand children. They enjoy bridge, reading, travel and luxury automobiles.

About Windstorm Creative
and our Readers' Club

Windstorm Creative was founded in 1989 to create a publishing house with author-centric ethics and cutting-edge, risk-taking innovation. Windstorm is now a company of more than ten divisions with international distribution channels that allow us to sell our books — paperback and hardcover — games, music and films both inside the traditional systems and outside these paradigms, capitalizing on more direct delivery and non-traditional markets. As a result, our books can be found in grocery superstores as well as your favorite neighborhood bookstore, and dozens of other outlets on and off the Internet.

Windstorm is an independent press with the synergy and branding of a corporate publisher and an author royalty that's easily twice their best offer. We have continued to minimize returns without decreasing sales by publishing books that are timeless, as opposed to timely, and never backlisting our books.

Windstorm is constantly changing, improving, and growing. We are driven by the needs of our authors – hailing from ten different countries – and the vision of our critically-acclaimed staff. All of our books are created with the strictest of environmental protections in mind. Our approach to no-waste, no-hazard, in-house production, and stringent out-source scrutiny, assures that our goals are met whether books are printed at our own facility or an outside press.

Because of these precautions, our books cost more. And though we know that our readers support our efforts, we also understand that a few dollars can add up. This is why we began our Readers' Club. Visit our webcenter and take 20% off every title, every day. No strings. No fine print.

While you're at our site, feel free to preview or request the first chapter of any of our titles, completely free of charge.

Thank you for supporting an independent press.

www.windstormcreative.com
and click on Shop

See next page for title recommendations.

Full Spectrum Information Library

America's Haunted Places Volume One:
Haunted America Speaks
(Dave Oester and Sharon Gill)
A fascinating journey to some of America's most haunted areas.

Baseball Bunting: The Lost Art
(Bobby Herb)
The history of bunting, fascinating facts and a how-to guide.

Condominiums
(Frank J. La Mar)
To buy or not to buy? Learn that the truth really is in the details.

Coping with a Loved One's Disease
(R. Anders Porter)
A partner's guide for dealing with a life-changing diagnosis.

Hand Percussion
(Jeff Kersh)
A wide variety of techniques for many hand drums.

Hiring the Right Candidate
(Kimberly Wylie)
How to find the perfect person for your organization.

Islam: The Facts
(Patricia Skinner)
An in-depth study of Islamic beliefs from spirituality to politics.

Singing Drummer: Add Vocals to Your Beat
(Kevin Ronkko)
Vital guide for percussionists who want to expand their vocal range.